Learning Network Forensics

Identify and safeguard your network against both internal and external threats, hackers, and malware attacks

Samir Datt

[PACKT] open source*
PUBLISHING   community experience distilled

BIRMINGHAM - MUMBAI

Learning Network Forensics

First published: February 2016

Production reference: 1230216

Published by Packt Publishing Ltd.
Livery Place
35 Livery Street
Birmingham B3 2PB, UK.

ISBN 978-1-78217-490-5

www.packtpub.com

Credits

Author
Samir Datt

Reviewers
Nikhil Agarwal
Clinton Dsouza

Commissioning Editor
Priya Singh

Acquisition Editor
Tushar Gupta

Content Development Editor
Riddhi Tuljapurkar

Technical Editor
Manthan Raja

Copy Editor
Vibha Shukla

Project Coordinator
Sanchita Mandal

Proofreader
Safis Editing

Indexer
Monica Ajmera Mehta

Graphics
Jason Monteiro
Kirk D'Penha

Production Coordinator
Conidon Miranda

Cover Work
Conidon Miranda

About the Author

Samir Datt has been dabbling with digital investigations since 1988, which was around the time he solved his first case with the help of an old PC and Lotus 123. He is the Founder CEO of Foundation Futuristic Technologies (P) Ltd, better known as `ForensicsGuru.com`. He is widely credited with evangelizing computer forensics in the Indian subcontinent and has personally trained thousands of law enforcement officers in the area. He has the distinction of starting the computer forensics industry in South Asia and setting up India's first computer forensic lab in the private sector. He is consulted by law enforcement agencies and private sector on various technology-related investigative issues. He has extensive experience in training thousands of investigators as well as examining a large number of digital sources of evidence in both private and government investigations.

At last it is done,

A journey that long ago was begun,

Many lights there are that have helped on the way,

To everyone of them, my thanks I would say.

This book would never have seen the light of day had it not been for Tushar Gupta, acquisition editor at Packt Publishing. He tracked me down and invited and convinced me to write. He encouraged me, cajoled me, and finally pushed me into the mystic world of authoring. Thanks Tushar!

I would also like to convey my heartfelt thanks to Riddhi Tuljapurkar, my content development editor. She has been a beacon guiding me through the myriad steps that being an author involves. A first-time author has many moments of self-doubt and hesitation; never did she let me falter, always encouraging, always supportive, she is perhaps the single most important reason that the book is ready on time. Thank you!

My book reviewers have been my compass and their encouragements, suggestions, comments, and guidance have been instrumental in getting the book to its present state. Thank you Clinton D'Souza and Nikhil Agarwal. I am indeed deeply grateful.

My family has been my biggest cheerleader. A special thanks to my wife, Resham, who has had to put up with my extensive travel schedules and uncounted holidays and weekends devoted to meeting the chapter deadlines. She has been my rock and has always believed that I was destined to write. My son, Madhav, who despite his own hectic schedules at IIT, Kharagpur, took time out to help me with the illustrations, screenshots, chapter editing, and scenario environments. Without you this could never have been done. Many thanks!

I also owe a thank you to my parents, who have been encouraging throughout the course of this book. My dogs, Tuffy, Lucky, Lolu, and Chutki, have been a source of inspiration by constantly bombarding me with unlimited doses of love and affection.

Thanks are also due to the rock-solid team at ForensicsGuru.com, who helped me with my research and chapter illustrations. Great work, guys!

Last but not least, I thank the Creator; for without Him, no creation is possible.

About the Reviewers

Nikhil Agarwal, an InfoSec researcher, proactive, and performance-driven professional from India with more than three years of progressive expertise in management and IT security field, is dedicated to operational excellence, quality, safety, and respectful leadership. Nikhil is insightful and result-driven IT professional with notable success directing a broad range of corporate IT security initiatives while participating in planning, analyzing, and implementing solutions in support of business objectives. He excels at providing comprehensive secure network design, systems analysis, and complete life cycle project management.

By qualification, Nikhil possesses a bachelor's degree in engineering in the domain of electronic and communications from Swami Keshvanand Institute of Technology, Management and Gramothan (SKIT) (http://www.skit.ac.in/), Jaipur, Rajasthan. He has completed various projects during his studies and submitted a range of research papers along with the highest range of international certifications. By profession, Nikhil is an IT security engineer and trainer, and a multi-faceted professional with more than three years of experience living, studying, and working in international environments (Asia and Africa). He has undertaken and successfully completed many security projects ranging from providing services, auditing, to training.

The description of his professional journey can be found on his LinkedIn profile (https://za.linkedin.com/in/reachatnikhil).

Nikhil spends much of his leisure time writing technical articles for his blogs, Technocrat Club (http://technocratclub.blogspot.com), and answering queries over Quora, Stack Overflow, and GitHub. He also has a passion for photography and travelling to new places. He enjoys authoring technical/nontechnical articles for various blogs and websites, along with reviewing books from various IT technologies.

Apart from this, Nikhil has founded and holds the post of President for a global non-profit organization, Youth Cross Foundation, working for socially-challenged people to bring up their quality of living with technology as their weapon.

Things that set Nikhil apart are creativity, passion, and honesty towards his work. He has always had the support of his family, friends, and relatives, especially his mother. From time to time, Nikhil holds seminars for organizations wanting to explore or discover the possibilities of information security and help answer the spatial questions better. Nikhil is also a lecturer and enjoys teaching the wonderful powers of IT security and explaining how to solve problems on various platforms to the students and corporates. Nikhil's work has also found special mentioning in some national news headlines (`http://www.thestatesman.com/mobi/news/features/checking-for-vulnerabilities/76087.html`).

Nikhil works over the ideology of Steve Jobs: *Stay Hungry. Stay Foolish.*

Clinton Dsouza is a technology analyst at Barclays in New York, NY. His current role involves analysis and development of security-related technologies in the Digital & IB Enterprise group. He holds bachelor's (B.S.) and master's (M.S.) degrees in computer science from Arizona State University (ASU), concentrating on information assurance and cybersecurity. His research at the Laboratory for Security Engineering for Future Computing (SEFCOM) at ASU was funded by Cisco and the U.S. Department of Energy (DOE). His projects involved access control for distributed systems and policy management for Internet of Things (IoT)-based computing ecosystems.

I would like to thank my professor and mentor at ASU, Dr. Gail-Joon Ahn, who guided and engaged me in the field of cybersecurity and information assurance. I would also like to thank my parents and friends for the motivation and inspiration to pursue a career in the field of cybersecurity.

www.PacktPub.com

eBooks, discount offers, and more

Did you know that Packt offers eBook versions of every book published, with PDF and ePub files available? You can upgrade to the eBook version at www.PacktPub.com and as a print book customer, you are entitled to a discount on the eBook copy. Get in touch with us at customercare@packtpub.com for more details.

At www.PacktPub.com, you can also read a collection of free technical articles, sign up for a range of free newsletters and receive exclusive discounts and offers on Packt books and eBooks.

https://www2.packtpub.com/books/subscription/packtlib

Do you need instant solutions to your IT questions? PacktLib is Packt's online digital book library. Here, you can search, access, and read Packt's entire library of books.

Why subscribe?

- Fully searchable across every book published by Packt
- Copy and paste, print, and bookmark content
- On demand and accessible via a web browser

Table of Contents

Preface

Just like the motto of the Olympic Games — *Faster, Higher, Stronger* — networks today are faster, wider, and greater. For widespread high-speed networks, carrying greater volumes of data has become a norm rather than the exception. All of these characteristics come with great exposure to a huge variety of threats to the data carried by the networks. The current threat landscape necessitates an increased understanding of the data on our networks, the way we secure it and the tell-tale signs left behind after an incident. This book aims at introducing the subject of network forensics to further help in understanding how data flows across the networks as well as introduce the ability to investigate forensic artifacts or clues to gather more information related to an incident.

What this book covers

Chapter 1, Becoming Network 007s, introduces the exciting world of network forensics. This chapter introduces the concepts and readies the reader to jump right into network forensics.

Chapter 2, Laying Hands on the Evidence, explains how to acquire both physical and virtual evidence in order to understand the type of incident involved.

Chapter 3, Capturing & Analyzing Data Packets, takes the user further into the world of network investigation by focusing on network traffic capture and analysis.

Chapter 4, Going Wireless, explains how to investigate wireless networks with additional considerations for wireless protection and security.

Chapter 5, Tracking an Intruder on the Network, investigates intrusions using a Network Intrusion Detection System (NIDS) and a Network Intrusion Prevention System (NIPS).

Chapter 6, Connecting the Dots – Event Logs, explains how to collect event logs and then correlate and connect the links, followed by the analysis.

Chapter 7, Proxies, Firewalls, and Routers, helps us to understand web proxies, firewalls, and routers and the reasons to investigate them.

Chapter 8, Smuggling Forbidden Protocols – Network Tunneling, shows advanced concepts of letting a network send its data via the connection of another network.

Chapter 9, Investigating Malware – Cyber Weapons of the Internet, covers advanced topics about the trends in malware evolution and the investigation of forensic artifacts caused by the malware.

Chapter 10, Closing the Deal – Solving the Case, enables the user with full-fledged skills in tackling cases to give the finishing touches and close the deal.

What you need for this book

Readers must be aware of the basics of operating systems such as Linux and Windows as well as networking concepts such as TCP/IP and routers.

The book uses the following software:

- Tcpdump with the libpcap library
- Wireshark
- FTK Imager (AccessData)
- NetworkMiner for passive network sniffing
- SNORT for evidence acquisition in the NIDS/NIPS mode
- Splunk to collect and analyze log files
- Squid as an open-source proxy
- YARA to help identify malware

Who this book is for

This book is intended for network administrators, system administrators, information security & forensics professionals, as well as the curious who wish to learn about network forensics and want to be able to identify, collect, examine, and analyze evidence that exists on the networks.

This could be from the perspective of internal threats, external intrusions, or a blend of both.

Further, this book will act as a great foundation for those interested in enhancing their skills and fast-tracking their career from both a personal and organizational growth perspective.

Conventions

In this book, you will find a number of text styles that distinguish between different kinds of information. Here are some examples of these styles and an explanation of their meaning.

Code words in text, database table names, folder names, filenames, file extensions, pathnames, dummy URLs, user input, and Twitter handles are shown as follows: "Tcpdump also provides the option to save the captured network traffic (packets) to a .pcap format file for future analysis."

Any command-line input or output is written as follows:

```
$ apt -get install tcpdump
```

New terms and **important words** are shown in bold. Words that you see on the screen, for example, in menus or dialog boxes, appear in the text like this: "The **Application** log stores events logged by the applications or programs."

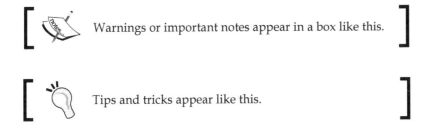

Warnings or important notes appear in a box like this.

Tips and tricks appear like this.

Reader feedback

Feedback from our readers is always welcome. Let us know what you think about this book—what you liked or disliked. Reader feedback is important for us as it helps us develop titles that you will really get the most out of.

To send us general feedback, simply e-mail feedback@packtpub.com, and mention the book's title in the subject of your message.

If there is a topic that you have expertise in and you are interested in either writing or contributing to a book, see our author guide at www.packtpub.com/authors.

Customer support

Now that you are the proud owner of a Packt book, we have a number of things to help you to get the most from your purchase.

Downloading the color images of this book

We also provide you with a PDF file that has color images of the screenshots/diagrams used in this book. The color images will help you better understand the changes in the output. You can download this file from `https://www.packtpub.com/sites/default/files/downloads/LearningNetworkForensics_ColorImages.pdf`.

Errata

Although we have taken every care to ensure the accuracy of our content, mistakes do happen. If you find a mistake in one of our books—maybe a mistake in the text or the code—we would be grateful if you could report this to us. By doing so, you can save other readers from frustration and help us improve subsequent versions of this book. If you find any errata, please report them by visiting `http://www.packtpub.com/submit-errata`, selecting your book, clicking on the **Errata Submission Form** link, and entering the details of your errata. Once your errata are verified, your submission will be accepted and the errata will be uploaded to our website or added to any list of existing errata under the Errata section of that title.

To view the previously submitted errata, go to `https://www.packtpub.com/books/content/support` and enter the name of the book in the search field. The required information will appear under the **Errata** section.

Piracy

Piracy of copyrighted material on the Internet is an ongoing problem across all media. At Packt, we take the protection of our copyright and licenses very seriously. If you come across any illegal copies of our works in any form on the Internet, please provide us with the location address or website name immediately so that we can pursue a remedy.

Please contact us at `copyright@packtpub.com` with a link to the suspected pirated material.

We appreciate your help in protecting our authors and our ability to bring you valuable content.

Questions

If you have a problem with any aspect of this book, you can contact us at `questions@packtpub.com`, and we will do our best to address the problem.

1
Becoming Network 007s

Welcome to the world of spies, glamor, high technology, and fast...

Wait a minute!

Are you sure you are reading the right book? Wasn't this book supposed to be about network forensics?

Yes, you are reading the right book!

Let me put you at ease. This is about network forensics. That said it also is a glamorous world full of high-tech spies and fast data (no cars, unfortunately). This is a world where the villains want to own the world (or at the very least, your digital world) and if they can't own it, they would like to destroy it.

This world needs a hero. A person who can track down spies, identify stolen secrets, beat the villains at their own game, and save the world in the bargain.

A tech-savvy, cool, and sophisticated hero! A digital 007! Come on, admit it, who doesn't fancy themselves as James Bond? Here's your chance, an opportunity to become a network 007.

Interested? Read on…

In this chapter, we will build an understanding of what we need to know in order to venture in the area of network forensics. We will cover the following topics here:

- 007 characteristics in the network world
- Identifying threats to the enterprise
- Data breach surveys
- Defining network forensics
- Differentiating between computer forensics and network forensics
- Strengthening our technical fundamentals
- Understanding network security
- Network security goals
- Digital footprints

007 characteristics in the network world

In 007's world, everything begins with a *trigger*. The trigger is an event or incident that alerts the organization about unsavory activities by persons known or unknown.

This could be reactive or proactive.

As part of its defense-in-depth defense strategy, an organization's network is protected by a number of preventive and detective (monitoring) controls. A trigger could be considered reactive in the case of an organization realizing that their competitors seem to be getting inside information, which is limited in circulation and extremely confidential in nature.

Similarly, a proactive trigger could be the result of an organization's authorized penetration testing and vulnerability assessment exercise.

Subsequent to a trigger event, a preliminary information-gathering exercise is initiated, which culminates in a briefing to the 007 (the investigator), outlining all the currently-known details of the breach/incident. Certain hypotheses are floated based on the information gathered so far. Possible cause and effect scenarios are explored. Likely internal and external suspects may be shortlisted for further investigation.

The investigator initiates a full-fledged information/evidence collection exercise using every sort of high-end technology available. The evidence collection may be done from network traffic, endpoint device memory, and hard drives of compromised computers or devices. Specialized tools are required to achieve this. This is done with the view of proving or disproving the hypotheses that were floated earlier. Just like a **closed-circuit television** (**CCTV**) camera or a spy cam that is used to collect information in real life, on a network, network traffic is collected using tools such as **Wireshark**, volatile memory data is collected by tools such as **Forensic Toolkit (FTK) Imager,** and media images are collected by tools such as **EnCase**.

The information collected is carefully and painstakingly analyzed with a view to extract evidence relating to the incident to help answer questions, as shown in the following diagram:

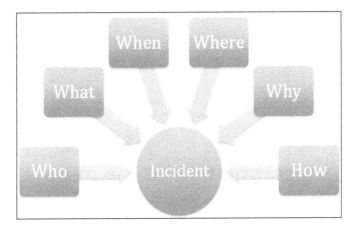

An attempt is made to answer the following critical questions:

- Who is behind the incident?
- What actually happened?
- When did it happen?
- Where was the impact felt? Or which resources were compromised?
- Why was it done?
- How was it done?

Based on the analysis result, a conclusion is drawn and certain recommendations are made. These recommendations result in an action. The action may include remediation, strengthening of defenses, employee/insider termination, prosecution of suspects, and so on based on the objectives of the investigation. The following flow diagram neatly sums up the complete process:

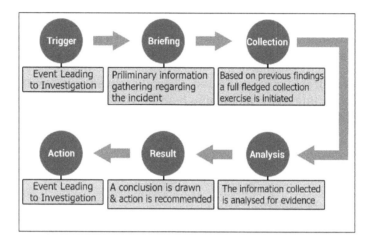

Bond characteristics for getting to satisfactory completion of the case

Network forensic investigations can be very time consuming and complex. These investigations are usually very sensitive in nature and can be extremely time critical as well. To be an effective network forensics Bond, we need to develop the following characteristics:

- **Preparation**: The preparation stage is essential to ultimately arrive at a satisfactory conclusion of a case. A calm thought-out response with a proper evidence-collection process comes from extensive training and the knowledge of what to do in the event of the occurrence of most likely scenarios that are happening in the real world. Practice leads to experience, which leads to the ability to innovate and arrive at out-of-the-box investigative insights for solving the case. A situation where the investigator is unable to identify a compromised system could lead to years of data theft, resulting in bleeding of the organization and its ultimate and untimely demise. A scenario where an investigator is able to identify the problem but is unable to decide what action to take is equally bad. This is where preparation comes in. The key is knowing what to do in most situations.

A clear-cut incident response plan needs to be in place. Trained personnel with the necessary tools and processes should be available to tackle any contingency. Just as organizations carry out fire drills on a regular basis, incident response drills should be institutionalized as part of the organization policy.

- **Information gathering/evidence gathering**: A comprehensive system to monitor network events & activity, store logs, and back them up is essential. Different inputs are generated by different event logging tools, firewalls, intrusion prevention & detection systems, and so on. These need to be stored and/or backed up at a secure location in order to prevent incidental or intentional tampering.

- **Understanding of human nature**: An understanding of human nature is critical. This helps the investigator to identify the modus operandi, attribute a motive to the attack, and anticipate and preempt the enemy's next move.

- **Instant action**: Just as Bond explodes into action at the slightest hint of danger, so must an investigator. Based on the preparations done and the incident response planned, immediate action must be taken when a network compromise is suspected. Questions such as *should the system be taken off the network?* or *should we isolate it from the network and see what is going on?* should be already decided upon at the planning stage. At this stage, time is of essence and immediate action is required.

- **Use of technology**: An investigator should have Bond's love of high technology. However, a thorough knowledge of the tools is a must. A number of hi-tech surveillance tools play an important role in network-based investigations. Specialized tools monitor network traffic, identify and retrieve hidden and cloaked data, analyze and visualize network logs and activities, and zero in on *in-memory* programs and malicious software and tools used by the bad guys.

- **Deductive reasoning**: A logical thought process, the ability to reason through all the steps involved, and the desire to see the case to its rightful conclusion are the skills that need to be a part of a network 007's arsenal. Questioning all the assumptions, questioning the unquestionable, understanding cause and effect, examining the likelihood of an event occurring, and so on are the hallmarks of an evolved investigator.

The TAARA methodology for network forensics

There is a considerable overlap between incident response and network forensics in the corporate world, with information security professionals being tasked with both the roles. To help simplify the understanding of the process, we have come up with the easy-to-remember **TAARA** framework:

- **Trigger**: This is the incident that leads to the investigation.

- **Acquire**: This is the process that is set in motion by the trigger—this is predefined as a part of the incident response plan—and it involves identifying, acquiring, and collecting information and evidence relating to the incident. This includes getting information related to the triggers, reasons for suspecting an incident, and identifying and acquiring sources of evidence for subsequent analysis.

- **Analysis**: All the evidence that is collected so far is collated, correlated, and analyzed. The sequence of events is identified. Pertinent questions such as whether the incident actually occurred or not; if it did, what exactly happened; how it happened; who was involved; what is the extent of the compromise; and so on are answered. Based on the information that is gathered during this stage, it may be necessary to go back to the acquire stage in order to gather additional evidence. Analysis is then initiated on the newly acquired evidence.

- **Report**: Based on the preceding analysis, a report is produced before the stakeholders in order to determine the next course of action.

- **Action**: The action recommended in the report is usually implemented during this stage.

This is pictorially represented in the following image:

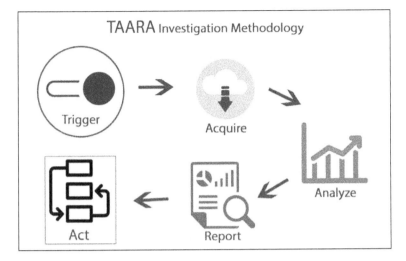

Identifying threats to the enterprise

Based on the source of the threat, attacks can be broadly classified into the following types:

- Internal
- External
- Hybrid

Internal threats

Threats or attacks that originate from within the network or organization are classified as internal threats. These can be intentional or unintentional.

Typically, such threats involve an insider with a mala fide intention, insider knowledge and/or access. This insider is looking to steal, misuse, modify, corrupt, or destroy enterprise resources. Quite naturally, the insider has no intention of getting caught and hence, makes every attempt to cover their tracks. However, as we will see later in this chapter, every interaction with the crime scene leaves a trace as per **Locard's exchange principle**.

Weak and ill-defined rules, network policies, security systems, and so on aid and abet such insiders. Unlimited and unmonitored access of network resources and data by the users are a sure recipe for disaster. Improperly implemented controls, random permissions, unsecured physical access to server rooms, and poor password hygiene contribute to serious threats to the network resources.

External threats

External threats are those that originate from outside the perimeter of the network. This could be from individuals, groups, or even governments. A spate of network attacks world-wide have been traced to state actors such as China, North Korea, and even the USA. Revelations by Snowden have opened everyone's eyes to the real threat of state-sponsored surveillance.

External threats come in all shapes and sizes. Just like internal threats, these can be intentional or unintentional. There are all sorts of people out there who want to get into your network. Some want to do it to get the information you store, some do it to shut down your network, some do it as they did not like the statement your company's CEO gave out last Wednesday, and some want to do it just because they can. Let's leave motivations aside for the moment. I say *for the moment* as a part of our network forensics investigations requires answering the *Why* part of the equation at a later date.

Any outsider wanting access to your network has to carry out a number of concrete steps before they can gain access of any sort. It's best to be disabused of the notion that, like in the movies, a hacker sits before his computer, starts typing, and has Administrator-level access within a couple of minutes. That is unadulterated fiction.

The first step any attacker has to take is to reconnoiter the target. Just as any good or accomplished thief will case the neighborhood to identify the potential targets, locate their weak spots, plan the right time to break in, and figure out a way to get in; any criminal with the intent to get into the network has to undergo a similar process. This process is called footprinting. This consists of a number of steps followed by scanning for open UDP & TCP ports, which can be exploited. An attempt is then made to try and get the password via multiple means such as social engineering, password lists, brute forcing, or rainbow tables. This mode of password discovery is the most difficult method of getting into the network. Another example would be to exploit the weakness such as unpatched OS and run programs that exploit a vulnerable software leading to open access, followed by privilege escalation to administrator level.

Once in, the accomplished spy will not do anything to give away the fact that they have administrator-level access. It is only script kiddies or publicity-hungry hackers that go ahead to deface websites to earn their two minutes of fame or notoriety.

The next objective is to create a backdoor for uninterrupted access and take every precaution to cover their tracks.

It can be months and, in some cases, years before an intrusion of such sort can be discovered or detected. That is the holy grail of the attacker. Spying undetected! Forever!

However, that is exactly where you come in, Mr. 007. You have to figure out what's going on in the network. At times, this needs to be done extremely covertly. Once the data breach is detected, you need to go into your *licensed to kill* mode to identify such intrusions and gather all the evidence of the related processes!

You need to identify the perpetrator, interrogate him or the witnesses (forensic interrogation of data packets, media, and memory) to identify the what, when, where, why, and how.

Intention → Source ↓	Intentional	Accidental
Internal	Insider data theft Insider sabotage Information leakage Assistance to outsiders Sexual harassment within the enterprise Tampering with sensitive data	Accidental assistance to outsiders Inadvertently letting malicious software loose on the network Unintentional use of compromised software on **bring your own device (BYOD)** Insiders social engineered to give away information such as passwords and so on
External	Targeted phishing or spear phishing to extract confidential information Network scans / OS fingerprinting / vulnerability assessments of outside-facing network components Denial of Service attacks State-sponsored surveillance	An outsider accidentally stumbling onto sensitive data because of a flaw/vulnerability in the network Accidental power outage Natural disasters An unsuspecting user's system can be taken over and used as part of a *bot herd*

Network threat examples

Data breach surveys

There are many data breach / information security / cyber crime surveys unfailingly published every year by the those of the consulting industry.

From a reference perspective, you may want to visit a few references on the net, listed as follows:

- The **Verizon Data Breach Investigations Report**: `http://www.verizonenterprise.com/DBIR/`

- PwC UK — **INFORMATION SECURITY BREACHES SURVEY 2014**: `http://www.pwc.co.uk/assets/pdf/cyber-security-2014-exec-summary.pdf`

- The Ponemon Institute's **Cost of Data Breach** Survey: `http://www.ponemon.org/blog/ponemon-institute-releases-2014-cost-of-data-breach-global-analysis`

- KPMG **Cybercrime survey report**: `https://www.kpmg.com/IN/en/IssuesAndInsights/ArticlesPublications/Documents/KPMG_Cyber_Crime_survey_report_2014.pdf`

- The InfoWatch **Global Data Leakage Report, 2014**: `http://infowatch.com/sites/default/files/report/InfoWatch_Global_data_leak_report_2014_ENG.pdf`

All of them point to a single unassailable fact — data breaches are becoming increasingly expensive and will continue to be so.

Some of the points brought up by most of them are:

- The cost of a data breach is on the rise.

- Post a breach — customers loose confidence and tend to change service providers. This is particularly common in the financial services industry.

- For many countries, malicious or criminal attacks are at the top spot as the root cause of the data breaches.

- In over 50% of the cases, insiders were involved in one way or the other.

What does this mean for us? It just means that we are in the right place at the right time. There will always be a very strong demand for the Sherlocks of the net. Professionals who can detect, collect, collate, analyze, and investigate will find themselves on the *must hire* list of most large-scale corporates.

Let's get started with the underlying principle of forensics of any sort.

Locard's exchange principle

No study of digital investigations can be considered well begun without an understanding of the underpinning of the science. Locard's exchange principle is the foundation on which scientific investigation methodologies are built.

Dr Edmond Locard (1877-1966) was a French scientist who worked with the French Secret Service in the First World War. He was a pioneer in forensic science and criminology. He developed a methodology to identify the nature and cause of death of French soldiers and prisoners by examining the wounds, damage stains, and other marks on the body.

He was known as the Sherlock Holmes of France.

He is often credited with saying *every contact leaves a trace*!

He speculated that anybody or anything that enters or leaves the crime scene (interaction with the crime scene) either leaves something behind or leaves with something from it (inadvertently or intentionally) and this can be used as forensic evidence. Let's consider a murder. Anybody that walks into a murder spot may leave the evidence of their presence in the form of footprints, fingerprints, and so on. Similarly, when someone leaves the crime scene, they may take specks of blood with them, local dust may adhere to their shoes, and so on.

How does this translate into the network world?

Essentially, every attempt to communicate with a device on the network leaves a trace somewhere; this could be at firewalls, intrusion detection systems, routers, event logs, and so on. Similarly, any attempt by an internal miscreant to access unauthorized resources will also leave a trace. This is depicted in the following image:

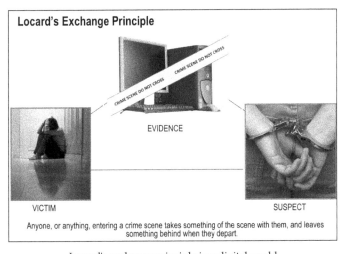

Locard's exchange principle in a digital world

Let's take the example of a phishing attack. As we are all aware, it begins with an innocuous mail with a massively appealing subject. The phishing mail may carry a payload in the form of an attachment (for example, a Trojan) or have a link that leads to a similar result. In this case, according to Locard's exchange principle, the two entities interacting would be the affected computer and the computer sending out the phish. Some of the evidence in this case would be the e-mail itself, Trojan horse/malware/keylogger, stolen passwords, changed passwords, attempts to cover tracks, and so on. The backdoor, once discovered, could reveal a lot of details and the IP addresses of devices that control it or receive the stolen data would also count as evidence. The command and control center for the phishing operation (if identified) would also be a goldmine of evidence.

As a network 007, it is our job to figure out what is going on and draw our conclusions accordingly.

Defining network forensics

What exactly is network forensics?

As per **National Institute of Standards and Technology** (**NIST**), *Digital forensics, also known as computer and network forensics, has many definitions. Generally, it is considered the application of science to the identification, collection, examination, and analysis of data while preserving the integrity of the information and maintaining a strict chain of custody for the data.*

Refer to `http://csrc.nist.gov/publications/nistpubs/800-86/SP800-86.pdf` for more information.

As per **WhatIs.com**, *network forensics is the capture, recording, and analysis of network events in order to discover the source of security attacks or other problem incidents.*

Broadly speaking, network forensics, in most people's perception, involves the CIA process. In this case, CIA stands for the following:

- Capture (capture packets)
- Identify (identify packets based on certain filtering criterion, such as date and time)
- Analyze (both known and unknown packets to understand what's going on)

The following image illustrates this:

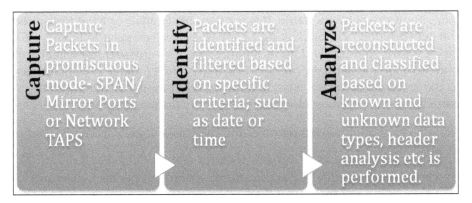

Broadly speaking, network forensics is the subset of digital forensics that deals with the investigation of events and activities related to digital networks. This involves monitoring and capturing network traffic and its related data from devices on the network with the objective of gathering evidence in a manner that is acceptable in the court of law.

Differentiating between computer forensics and network forensics

Network forensics is a branch of digital forensics. That said; it is significantly different from conventional forensic investigations. It is necessary to highlight the differences so that things are a lot clearer in the network investigator's mind.

Unlike other areas of digital forensics, network forensic investigations deal with volatile and dynamic information. Disk or computer forensics primarily deals with data at rest. The simplified normal process is to identify the media that to be investigated, create and authenticate a forensic image, identify the different artifacts to be investigated, carry out an in-depth analysis, and follow it up with a report highlighting the findings. Usually, these can include deleted, misnamed, and hidden files and artifacts; registry entries; password-protected files; e-mail communications; carved data; and so on. However, all these represent the state of the system at the time of the collection and imaging. This is what we call a post-mortem investigation (this does not include live-memory forensics, which, as the name suggests, is very much alive).

Network forensics by its very nature is dynamic. In fact, it would not be possible to conduct a network forensic investigation if prior arrangements were not made to capture and store network traffic. It is not possible to analyze what transpired with the network flow without having a copy of it. This is similar to having a CCTV footage for a particular incident. In its absence, one can only surmise what happened based on other circumstantial evidence. When the actual footage is available, as long as the investigator knows what to look for, the complete incident can be reconstructed and it becomes a lot easier to identify the perpetrator.

Additionally, network forensics involves the analysis of logs. This can be a bit of art as well as science.

Usually various network devices, applications, operating systems in use, and other programmable and intelligent devices on the network generate logs. Logs are time-sequenced. They can be quite cryptic in nature and different devices will address the same event in different ways. Some operating systems will call a login action as a login; whereas, another device may call it a log on and a third may call it a user authentication event. The message content and syntax of logs are vendor-specific. It may also vary from application to application.

Disk forensics does not have these sorts of intricacies. While logs exist and do vary across applications and operating systems, the level of dependency on logs in the case of disk forensics is not as high as that of network forensics.

That said, all disk, network, and memory forensics go hand in hand. Most investigations may involve at least a few, if not all, of the disciplines of digital forensics in any case of a reasonable magnitude.

In fact, a case where disk forensics is not used in an investigation could be considered equivalent to a conventional case where CCTV evidence has been overlooked.

Strengthening our technical fundamentals

Before we develop our skills on network forensics, we need to have certain basic fundamentals in place.

A network, in general parlance, is a group of computers/devices that are connected to each other. The connection could be wired or wireless. Every device on the network has a unique network address. This can be temporary (session specific) or permanent. Addresses are numeric quantities that are easy for computers to work with; however, they are not for humans to remember. These are known as IP addresses. For example 206.166.240.9. Consider the following diagram:

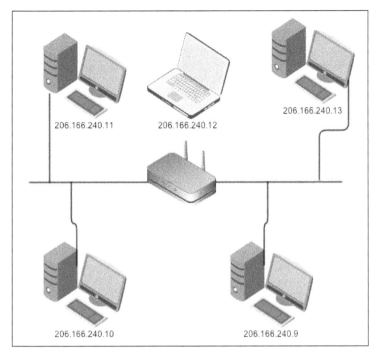

A simple network

To make these numeric addresses easy for humans to remember, they are stored as textual addresses as **Domain Name Server (DNS)** records. DNS servers are responsible for translating textual Internet addresses into numeric Internet addresses.

While numeric IP addresses identify a specific host machine working on a network, a numeric port number is used to identify specific processes that are running on a host machine. The number of ports is not functionally limited. Some of the common ports are as follows:

Port number	Application
20	FTP
21	FTP
23	Telnet
25	SMTP (mail)
79	Finger
80	HTTP
110	POP3 (mail)
443	HTTPS

When devices are connected to each other; they can communicate. The mode of communication between devices is via exchange of data. Data is transferred using *packet switching*. Messages are broken into packets and transmitted over the network. Each of these packets have a specified maximum size, and are split in to a header and data area. As each packet is being sent from a source computer to a destination computer or device, their addresses and the information that is necessary to properly sequence the packets at the reconstruction stage is included in the header.

Communications between two connected computers on a network are governed by rules known as protocols.

Protocols define the following:

- Addressing of messages
- Routing of messages
- Error detection
- Error recovery
- Packet sequence
- Flow controls

Protocol design is based on a layered architecture model such as the **Open Systems Interconnection (OSI)** reference model.

This is also known as the seven-layer model.

The seven-layer model

As the name suggests, this model consists of seven layers. Each of these are explained in the following:

- Layer 1: This is called the **physical layer**. This is the actual physical infrastructure over which the data travels. This consists of the cables, hubs, and so on. This is the electronics that ensures the physical transmission and reception of raw and unstructured bits and bytes.
- Layer 2: This is called the **data link layer**. This layer is responsible for the data encapsulation in the form of packets and their interpretation at the physical layer. This will initiate and terminate a logical link between two nodes on a network. Layer 2 is responsible for error-free transfer of data over the physical layer.

- Layer 3: This is called the **network layer**. This layer is in charge of a packet's transmission from a source to its destination. This layer decides the route, mapping of the logical and physical addresses, and data traffic control.

- Layer 4: This is called the **transport layer**. The transport layer is in charge of the delivery of the packets from a source to a destination. This ensures that the message is delivered in a sequence without duplication or loss and is error-free.

- Layer 5: This is called the **session layer**. The session layer manages the network access. It establishes sessions among the processes running on different nodes via different logical ports. Layer 5 also handles session establishment, maintenance, and termination.

- Layer 6: This is called the **presentation layer**. The role of the presentation layer is to format the data transmitted to applications, data conversion, compressing/decompressing, encrypting, and so on. This allows access to end user for various Windows services such as resource sharing, remote printing, and so on.

- Layer 7: This is called the **application layer**. This is the end user layer. This layer contains the applications, such as Java, Microsoft Word, and so on, that are used by the end user.

As the data travels between layers, each layer adds or removes its header to the data unit. At the destination, each added header is removed one-by-one until the receiving application gets the data that is intended for it.

The TCP/IP model

The TCP/IP model consists of only four layers. These are application, transport, internet, and network.

These layers are shown in the following table:

Layer Name	Description
Application	This is responsible for applications and processes running on the network
Transport	This provides end-to-end data delivery
Internet	This makes datagrams and handles data routing
Network	This allows access to the physical network

Let's take a look at each of these one by one, starting from the network interface layer and working our way upwards.

- **Network layer**: The network (or network interface layer, as it is also known) is the bedrock of the TCP/IP model. This drives the signals across the network. It transmits and receives bits over the network hardware such as co-axial or twisted pair copper cable. This exists over the physical layer and includes the following protocols:

  ° Ethernet

  ° Token-ring

  ° Frame relay

  ° FDDI

  ° X.25

  ° RS-232

  ° v.35

- **Internet layer**: The Internet layer is at the heart of the TCP/IP model. This packages the data into IP datagrams and performs routing for these datagrams based on the source and destination information in the header. The protocols used at this layer include the following:

  ° **Internet Protocol (IP)**

  ° **Internet Control Message Protocol (ICMP)**

  ° **Address Resolution Protocol (ARP)**

  ° **Reverse Address Resolution Protocol (RARP)**

- **Transport layer**: This layer manages the communication session between the host computers. During the data transportation process, this defines the level of service and the connection status. The transport layer uses the following protocols:

  ° **Transmission Control Protocol (TCP)**

  ° **User Datagram Protocol (UDP)**

  ° **Real-time Transport Protocol (RTP)**

- **Application layer**: The application layer combines the functions of the OSI application, presentation, and session layers. This layer defines how the host programs interface with transport layer services as well as their related application protocols. Some of the protocols in this layer are as follows:

  ○ **Simple Mail Transfer Protocol (SMTP)**

  ○ HTTP

  ○ FTP

  ○ Telnet

  ○ **Simple Network Management Protocol (SNMP)**

  ○ DNS

  ○ **Trivial File Transfer Protocol (TFTP)**

  ○ X-Windows

The following image depicts both models in graphic form. It also shows their interrelation:

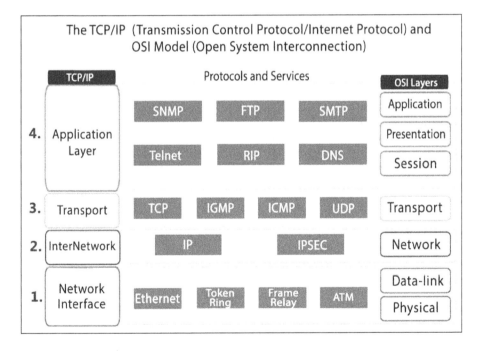

Understanding the concept of interconnection between networks/Internet

In 1966, the Defense Advanced Research Project Agency Network, implemented a research network of networks. This consisted of connecting several computer networks based on different protocols.

This threw up a unique problem of having to define a common interconnection protocol on top of the local protocols. The **Internet Protocol (IP)** plays this role by defining unique addresses for a network device and host machines. The following diagram depicts this interconnection of devices using IP routing:

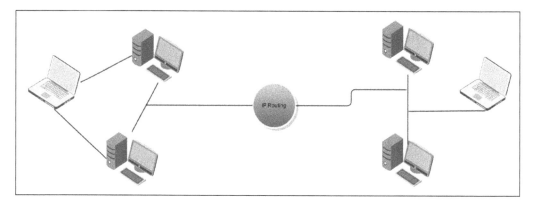

Internet Protocol (IP)

Whenever we see a stranger that we want to speak to, it always helps if we speak the same language. In computer world, the language of communication is called a protocol. IP is one of the languages that multiple computers use to communicate with each other as a part of the layered architecture model.

On top of the IP, there are TCP, UDP, and some others.

There are two versions of the IP being used, as follows:

- **Internet Protocol version 4 (IPv4)**
- **Internet Protocol version 6 (IPv6)**

The Internet Protocol has the following two main functions:

- Splitting the data stream into standard size packets at the source and then putting them together again in the correct order at the destination.
- Guiding or routing a packet through a number of intermediary networks, starting from the source device IP address to the destination device IP address.

How does it work?

It splits or breaks up the initial data (that is to be sent) into datagrams. Each datagram will have a header, including the IP address and the port number of the destination. Datagrams are then sent to selected gateways, that is, IP routers. These routers are connected to the local network and to an IP service provider network at the same time. These routers start the relay process, wherein datagrams are transferred from gateway to gateway until they arrive at their final destination.

The following diagram illustrates this concept in a simple-to-understand manner:

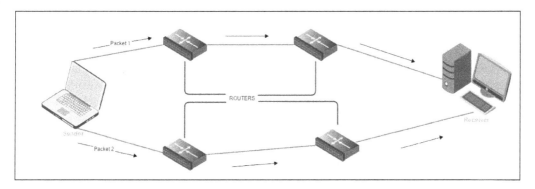

Whenever two hosts communicate with each other using the Internet Protocol, there is no need for a continuous connection. One host sends the data to another via a data packet. Each packet header contains the source destination addresses as well as the sequence number and is treated as an independent unit of data. The TCP is responsible for reading the packet headers and putting the packets in the correct sequence so that the message is readable.

Today, the most widely used version of IP is the IPv4. However, IPv6 is also beginning to be supported. IPv6 was introduced when it was realized that IPv4 addresses were running out. The exponential increase in the number of devices connected to the Internet resulted in the anticipation of IPv4 address exhaustion. IPv6 provides for much longer addresses and also the possibility of many more Internet users. IPv6 includes the capabilities of IPv4 and any server that can support IPv6 packets can also support IPv4 packets.

Structure of an IP packet

Let's take a look at the following structure of an IP packet:

- The IP's functionality and limitations are defined by the fields at the beginning of the packet. This is called the frame header.

- The source and destination address fields have 32 bits allocated to encode their data.

- Various additional information, such as the total packet length in bytes, is encoded in 16 bytes in the remainder of the header.

Normally, the application layer sends the data that is to be transmitted to the transport layer. The transport layer adds a header and sends it to the Internet layer. The Internet layer adds its own header to this and sends it to the network layer for physical transmission in the form of an IP datagram. The network layer adds its own frame header and footer and then physically transmits it over the network.

At the other end, when the datagram is received, this process is reversed and the different headers are stripped as the data moves from layer to layer. The following diagram represents how headers are added and removed as we move from layer to layer:

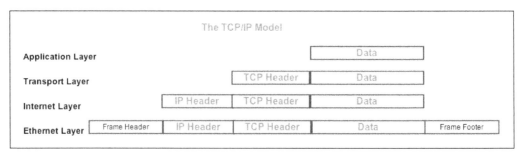

Datagram headers as we move from layer to layer

Transmission Control Protocol (TCP)

IP packets are a basic service that do not guarantee safe delivery. TCP remedies this by adding the following elements:

- Error detection

- Safe data transmission

- Assurance that data is received in the correct order

Before sending the data, TCP requires the computers that are communicating to establish a connection with each other:

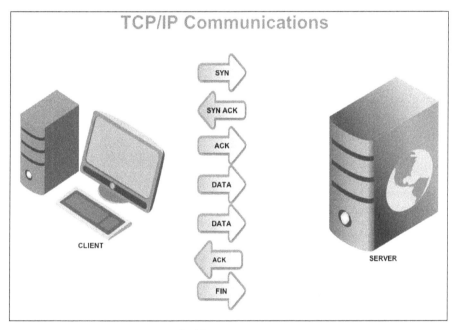

TCP/IP communications

Whereas IP is limited to sending 64-kb data streams, large data streams can be sent as one big stream of data using TCP. TCP does this by breaking up the data stream into separate data packets. Each packet is numbered and its sequence number is stored in the header. On arrival, these disparate packets are reassembled using sequence and sequence acknowledgement numbers. TCP specifies the port numbers. This improves the capabilities over IP. Every TCP/IP machine can communicate using 65,536 different ports or sockets.

All data in a TCP packet is accompanied by a header. The header contains information related to the source port, destination port, sequence number, sequence acknowledgement number, and some miscellaneous header data.

User Datagram Protocol (UDP)

Similar to the TCP, the UDP is also built on top of the IP. It has the same packet-size limit (64 kb) as IP; however, it allows specifying port numbers. This provides 65,536 different ports, which is the same as TCP. Therefore, every machine has two sets of 65,536 ports: one for TCP and the other for UDP.

The difference between the two is that UDP is a connection-less protocol, without any error detection facility. It only provides support for data transmission from one end to other without any verification. As it does not do any further verification, UDP is very fast. This is its main feature and it is extremely useful in sending small and repetitive data at a very high speed. Some examples of this are audio and video streaming, games, time information that is continuously streamed, and so on.

Internet application protocols

On top of the TCP/IP layers is the application layer. The **Internet Engineering Task Force (IETF)** definition document for the application layer in the Internet protocol suite is **RFC 1123**. The application layer's role is to support network applications by the means of application protocols.

Some of the application protocols include the following:

- Telnet: This is a text input-based protocol that allows the user to perform a remote login on another computer
- **File Transfer Protocol (FTP)**: This is for the file transfer
- SMTP: This is for the transportation of electronic mail
- DNS: This is for the networking support
- SNMP: This is for the remote host management
- **Hypertext Transfer Protocol (HTTP)**
- **Network News Transfer Protocol (NNTP)**: This is allow the users to create news groups around specific subjects

Newer applications can also spawn additional application protocols such as BitTorrent, Bitcoin, eDonkey, and so on.

Understanding network security

We live in a wired world (could be wireless too), which is increasingly interconnected. These interconnected networks are privy to most of the world's data, which is at great risk.

Today, the more interconnected we are, the more at risk we are. With attacks of increasing sophistication becoming automated, easily available, and usable by most low-grade criminals, the threat to our resources is at an all-time high. Evolved and sophisticated detection-evasion techniques help in making things even more complicated. Criminals too have learned to follow the money. Attacks are more focused and targeted with a preponderance of effort being directed towards the targets that could result in a monetary payoff.

Let's take a look at the type of threats that exist.

Types of threats

When we connect our network to the outside world (I know, I know, we have to!), we introduce the possibility of outsiders attempting to exploit our network, stealing our data, infecting our systems with viruses and Trojans, or overloading our servers, thus impacting and impeding our performance.

However, if our network were disconnected from the outside world, threats would still exist. In fact, most surveys and studies (as mentioned earlier) point to the indisputable fact that most of the threats (over 50%) are caused by intentional or unintentional activities performed by insiders.

While it is rarely possible to isolate or *air gap* a business network from the outside world, even if we were to do so, there is no guarantee that it would ensure network security.

Based on this understanding, we must consider both internal and external threats.

Internal threats

Looking back at the history, we will see many notable examples of entire kingdoms being lost due to the actions of the insiders. Valuable information such as hidden routes to reach behind an army (backdoors), type, strengths & weaknesses of the defenses (scans & vulnerabilities), and access codes and passwords (open sesame) when leaked to the enemy can cause irreparable loss. Kingdoms and corporations can fall. Sun Tzu, the ancient Chinese strategist and general, in his martial treatise, **The Art of War**, strongly recommends the use of *insiders* to win battles. His opinion on the best way to win a battle is without firing a single shot.

Threats that originate from within the network tend to be way more serious than those that originate outside.

Just like an unknown enemy within the walls of a citadel can be lethal; similarly, the insider within your network can be very damaging unless identified and contained very quickly.

Insiders usually have plenty of knowledge about the network, its available resources, and structure. They already have been granted a certain level of access in order to be able to do their job. Network security tools such as firewalls, **intrusion prevention systems (IPS)**, **intrusion detection system (IDS)**, and so on are deployed at the periphery of the network and are usually outward facing and such insiders are *under the radar* in this context.

An insider can steal information in many low-tech ways. Simply inserting a USB drive and copying data off the network is a very common way of stealing data. Burning a DVD with the organization's intellectual property and walking off the premises with this stuck inside a laptop's DVD drive happens quite often. Some smart guys copy the data onto a USB stick and then delete it so that when checked, they can demonstrate that the USB device is empty and once they get home, they can then recover the data using free recovery tools.

A single insider can be quite dangerous; however, when there are multiple insiders working in tandem, the situation can be quite grave. These threats need to be addressed and mitigated quickly in order to prevent substantial damage.

External threats

Usually, external attackers do not have in-depth knowledge of your network. When they start out, they do not have login or access credentials to get into the network.

Once a potential target is identified, the first step is to carry out a reconnaissance on the network. To do this, they perform a ping sweep. This helps in identifying the IP addresses that respond to the pings and are accessible from the outside. Once these IP addresses are identified, a port scan is performed. The objective is to identify open services on these IP addresses. The **operating system (OS)** is fingerprinted to understand the make, model, and build deployed. This helps the attacker in identifying the possible unpatched vulnerabilities. An outsider will identify and exploit a known vulnerability to compromise any one of the earlier discovered services on the host. Once the attacker has gained access to the host, the attacker will work at escalating the privileges, covering tracks, and creating backdoors for future unmonitored access. They will then use this system as a platform to attack and compromise other systems in this network and the world at large.

Network security goals

In today's high-speed, always-on-the-go world, no man is an island. The same is the case with corporate networks. Constant communications and contact with the outside world, cloud-based applications, cloud and offsite storage of data, and BYOD lead to an increasingly connected network environment. A global economy that thrives on information, advanced technology that enables seamless transactions, and the constant human need to access information that is online are the factors leading to higher security risks.

Today, one can safely assume that most corporate networks are interconnected with other networks.

These networks run standards-based protocols.

These networks will also have a number of applications, which may have proprietary protocols. As such applications are bespoke, the focus of the developers is more on functionality and less on security. Further, there is no regular system of patching vulnerabilities in these applications.

The multitude of connected devices and diverse applications in corporate networks are quite complex and their volume is constantly increasing.

From a network security perspective, the primary goals are as follows:

- Confidentiality
- Integrity
- Availability

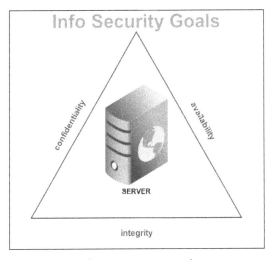

Information security goals

Confidentiality

The data that resides on the networks is the lifeblood of any organization. The confidentiality aspect of network security involves keeping the data private.

This entails restricting physical access to the networked devices and components as well as logical access to the node data and network traffic.

To do this, network administrators set up firewalls and intrusion detection & prevention systems. **Access control lists** (**ACL**) prevent unauthorized access to the network resources. Encrypted network traffic prevents any data leakage caused by traffic interception by an attacker. Specific credentials, such as usernames and passwords, are required to access the network resources.

Snowden's revelations are an example of a breach of the confidentiality goal of network security. The recent headlines relating to the data leakage at Sony Pictures is another glaring example.

Integrity

Networks have data in motion. Should an attacker gain access to a network, they would have the ability to silently modify/tamper with the traffic that would cause, at the very least, a misunderstanding between the people communicating and at the other end of the spectrum, it could cause irreparable harm to the people and organizations.

The examples of network security violations that affect the integrity goal include the following:

- Interception of communications related to electronic payments, modifying them to reflect different bank details, and diverting the payment from the unsuspecting remitter. This is a common problem that is being observed these days, especially between small-scale exporters and their buyers.

- A government taxation entity had their website compromised. The attacker very carefully only modified the section relating to tax rates. These were substantially reduced. As a result, the government lost substantial revenues as most of the remittances were made as per the rates posted on the website.

A number of organizations deploy a data integrity solution to perform origin authentication and verify that the traffic is originating from the source that should be sending it.

Availability

Data at rest and in transit is actually performing a task for the organization. As long as this data or information is accessible to authorized and authenticated users, the task can be performed. The moment an incident interrupts the access, preventing the users from performing their tasks, the availability goal of network security is breached.

There have been a number of high-profile examples of availability compromise in the past, as shown in the following:

- On April 26, 2007, Estonia, a small Baltic state experienced a wave of **denial-of-service** (**DoS**) attacks. These cyber attacks were launched as a protest against the Estonian government's removal of the Bronze Soldier monument in Tallinn. This was erected in 1947 as a Soviet World War II war monument. The effect was felt on a number of institutions, including banks, government, and universities, taking the network resources offline. This attack lasted for three weeks and shook the whole country. In fact, one of the repercussions of this attack was the formation of the US government's policy on cyber war.

- A very popular example was demonstrated in the movie Die Hard 4 — Live Free or Die Hard — where super cop, John McClane took on an Internet-based terrorist, who worked at systematically attacking and shutting down the United States government, transport, and economy. This movie is widely credited for adding the word **Fire Sale** to the vocabulary of the common man in a cyber context.

Today, some of the most common attacks compromising the availability goal are flood attacks, logic/software attacks, mail bombing, DoS attacks, accidental DoS attacks, and **distributed denial-of-service** (**DDoS**) attacks.

How are networks exploited?

Just as all humans have weaknesses, networks too have weaknesses. These are known as vulnerabilities. Vulnerability, in an information system, is a weakness that an attacker leverages to gain unauthorized access to the system or its data.

The usual modus operandi to take advantage of a network vulnerability is to write a program that does this. These kind of programs are called exploits. Most exploits are malicious in nature. As the name suggests, an exploit is meant to exploit the system's weakness.

Vulnerabilities can be of many types. Some examples are shown as follows:

- Physical vulnerabilities or natural disasters (such as, the tsunami in Southeast Asia)
- Network design vulnerabilities
- Network configuration vulnerabilities
- Protocol vulnerabilities
- Application vulnerabilities
- Targeted vulnerabilities such as malicious software
- Standard operating procedure/controls vulnerabilities
- Physical security vulnerabilities
- Human vulnerabilities

As we are all aware, a chain is only as strong as its weakest link. In the case of network security, the weakest link is usually human. Statistics show that an insider usually launches the most amount of attacks against information assets. Thus, most organizations set up controls to prevent insider abuse.

Digital footprints

For a moment, let's flashback to the *Locard's exchange principle* section. To reiterate, it basically expounds that *every contact leaves a trace*. What this means, in the digital context, is that all interactions with the digital system/network will leave some sort of an artifact/data behind as evidence of this event. These artifacts are known as digital footprints. They are of the following two types:

- Passive
- Active

Passive digital footprints are created by the system without the knowledge of the user, such as in the case of pasting passwords from a file to an application evidence or copies can be found in the volatile memory. Cookies are another example of this.

The user creates active digital footprints deliberately, such as in the case of a Facebook post, sending an e-mail, or storing and transmitting pictures.

These will usually exist and can be recovered from the following:

- Device memory
- Disk space including logs
- Network traffic capture

Summary

Our journey into the realm of network forensics has begun. We started out by identifying the characteristics that would make us 007 in the network forensics world. This was followed by learning about the TAARA methodology for investigations. We also learned about the various threats to an enterprise while strengthening our technical fundamentals. By the end of the chapter, we deepened our understanding of network security as well as network forensics.

In the next chapter, we will learn how to identify the different sources of evidence that are essential for a network forensic investigation. We will also learn how to collect and safely handle the evidence. So...let's get started!!!

2
Laying Hands on the Evidence

"Unless you know where you are going, you won't know how to get there!"

– Neil Strauss, The Rules of the Game

In this chapter, you will learn how to identify the different sources of evidence and get your hands on the evidence. You will learn how to acquire, manage, and handle the evidence to understand how a crime was committed.

The chapter will cover the following topics:

- Identifying sources of evidence
- Learning to handle the evidence
- Collecting network traffic using tcpdump
- Collecting network traffic using Wireshark
- Collecting network logs
- Acquiring memory using FTK Imager

Identifying sources of evidence

For any successful investigation, it is extremely important to successfully collect, collate, preserve, and analyze the evidence.

To begin with, we need to identify the sources of evidence for any investigation.

The sources of evidence can be easily divided into the following two categories:

Evidence obtainable from within the network

Consider the following image:

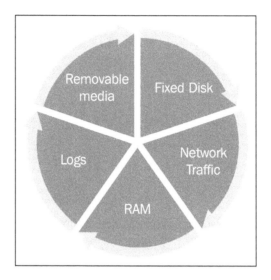

This can include the following:

- Evidence from network & device logs:

    A log is a record of all the activities and outcomes performed by a device or by outside agents on a device. Thus, all the incoming or outgoing events are logged on a system. Logs are a crucial part of the investigation ecosystem.

    Devices such as firewalls, intrusion prevention and detection systems, anti-virus servers, and so on generate logs. Other logs include operating system event logs, application logs, and so on.

- Network traffic:

    As discussed in the previous chapter, network traffic is transmitted in packets. The data is split up and transmitted in the form of packets that need to be captured and reconstructed for analysis.

- Memory of the individual computers under investigation:

    Volatile memory can be a valuable source of evidence. A lot of malware may only reside in the memory of a computer, which is under investigation. Similarly, computers with **whole disk encryption (WDE)** may save the key on a USB stick and the key will only be accessible to the investigator if it is grabbed from the volatile memory. Any kind of investigation that involves memory will require us to acquire the data from the suspect system's memory.

- Evidence residing on the hard drives of individual computers under investigation:

  Substantial evidential data resides on the hard drives of compromised computers. Traces of internet activity, web mail communications, efforts to cover tracks and obfuscate evidence, and so on will all be found post an investigation of hard drive contents. The registry of Windows computers is also a treasure trove of information. A bit stream image has to be obtained for each drive under investigation.

Evidence from outside the network

This can include the following:

- **Internet service provider (ISP) logs:**

  These logs are a detailed record of access to various Internet resources that are provided by the ISP. This can include details related to log on, log off, user names, resources accessed, online content, online activity, IP addresses, date and time of usage, as well as the duration of usage.

- Domain name controller logs:

  The domain name controller logs may also include date and time, IP addresses, queried domain names, protocol used, and so on. This data is usually available for a very short period of time due to the high volume of data in the logs as well as the log rotation policies followed by the service provider.

- Internet archives (Wayback Machine):

  These are online resources that archive websites and pages for a specific period of time. This can help us to determine the state of an Internet server offering up websites before a defacement attack. The URL to the Wayback Machine is `http://archive.org/web/`.

- Domain hosting provider logs:

  These are servers that host a domain. Unauthorized attempts to log in to the domain host are all logged here. A log of the activities of, for example, a criminal attempting to hack in would be available with this machine.

- Evidence on mobile devices:

  When hand-held devices such as phones or tablets are used to access network resources, evidence of their interaction is created on these devices. This too may be required from an investigation perspective.

A number of these sources of evidence may be protected by privacy laws and may not be easily available to the company investigators without a formal request from the law enforcement officers or a subpoena.

Further along in this chapter, we will discuss the tools and the methodology required to acquire the evidence from network packets and system memory in a step-by-step manner for further analysis.

Learning to handle the evidence

Once the sources of evidence are identified, the next critical aspect is to learn how to handle the evidence. In the previous chapter, we saw that forensics involves investigative processes used in a manner that is acceptable to a court of law.

Therefore, we need to ensure that all processes followed by us do not compromise the evidentiary value of the collected information.

Rules for the collection of digital evidence

Digital evidence, by its very nature, is fragile. It is extremely easy to tamper with and equally easy to destroy it.

In fact, in the early days, one of the key features that made computers so popular was the fact that a document that was made in a word processor could be very easily modified and mass produced.

In an evidentiary world, this means that whenever we handle the evidence or transport digital evidence, we may cause it to change. In fact, we may cause the digital evidence to change even when viewing it. Digital evidence may also degrade over time. This can be caused by the physical degradation of the media that the evidence is stored on. In fact, a single out-of-place bit can cause a substantial dent in our watertight case, raising questions about its authenticity and its admissibility, ultimately.

To ensure that this does not happen, as investigators, we need to adhere to a set of fundamental rules.

Rule 1: never mishandle the evidence

As discussed earlier, evidence has to be handled with extreme care. The objective is to minimize any disruptive contact with the evidence. When it is essential for the investigator to interact with the evidence, it must be done in a manner that is least intrusive and completely documented.

Rule 2: never work on the original evidence or system

Any interaction with the original evidence in digital form causes the evidence to be compromised. Metadata such as dates and time stamps on files change almost instantly. Unless the original evidence is handled in a *write-blocked* manner, the possibility of the evidence being compromised is a real threat to the successful completion of the case.

Conversely, the suspect system should never be used to carry out an investigation. Not only does that compromise the evidence, but it also adds to the risk of the evidence being manipulated / deleted / damaged / destroyed.

The recommended process is to create a forensic copy of the digital evidence, ensure its authenticity vis-à-vis the original, then carry out further investigations that are required in a write-protected manner.

Rule 3: document everything

In an investigation, any evidence is only as good as the process followed to obtain it. Unless proper processes with the correct precautions are followed, the process of acquiring and authenticating the evidence may be flawed until we have a clear-cut documentation attesting to the fact.

Therefore, the *cradle-to-grave* documentation for all the exhibits and authenticated images of the exhibits is a must. A comprehensive **chain of custody**, or **CoC** as it is known, has to be followed, where a detailed record is to be maintained vis-à-vis every exhibit and who had it in custody at any specific period of time. Hash values should be maintained and rechecked every time the exhibit changes hands.

At this point, it is appropriate to lay an increased emphasis on the CoC documentation process. CoC is a critical part of the investigation process. It documents every step and stage that a piece of evidence goes through in great detail. It maintains a record of every custodian (person) who was in possession of the evidence item at any point of time since the time of it being tagged as a part of the case under investigation.

Any discrepancies or gaps in the CoC can be a cause for dismissal of the case. Therefore, a CoC is considered to be as important as the case evidence itself. This is something that every investigator needs to keep in mind while conducting a forensic examination.

Collecting network traffic using tcpdump

Tcpdump is a command-line tool that runs on various flavors of Linux. It can be used for network traffic packet capture and analysis. It is a free tool that is distributed under the **Berkeley Software Distribution** (**BSD**) license.

Tcpdump requires the **libpcap** library to capture packets. Tcpdump has also been ported to Windows. In this avatar, it requires the **WinPcap** library, which is a port of libpcap for Windows.

Tcpdump is a great tool to learn about the traffic on your network in a more hands-on way. Though tcpdump requires more inputs from the user vis-à-vis higher analysis tools such as Wireshark, it really increases your fundamental understanding of the TCP/IP suite. Any security professional getting in the network forensics domain must understand the data in its raw form.

Tcpdump also provides the option to save the captured network traffic (packets) to a `.pcap` format file for future analysis.

From a learning perspective, we will use tcpdump with libpcap to grab network traffic.

Before we get started on the hands-on aspect, we will require the following prerequisites:

- A system running Linux (a VM with Linux will also do). We will be using Ubuntu on our system.
- A download of tcpdump and libpcap—both available at `http://www.tcpdump.org/`.

Let's get started.

Installing tcpdump

Before we can get going with capturing network traffic, we need to prepare our system and ourselves by having all our tools installed and configured for use.

As a rule, tcpdump comes pre-installed on most Linux distributions; however, just for the sake of completeness, we will see how to install it, as shown in the following image:

Open the terminal and run the following command to install tcpdump:

```
$ apt-get install tcpdump
```

Before we can actually use tcpdump, we need to understand the various tcpdump commands and options.

Understanding tcpdump command parameters

Tcpdump comes with a large number of parameters that inform it what to do. The best source of information for all of the tcpdump command-line options is its man page.

At the terminal prompt, type the following:

```
$ man tcpdump
```

The output is as shown in the following screenshot:

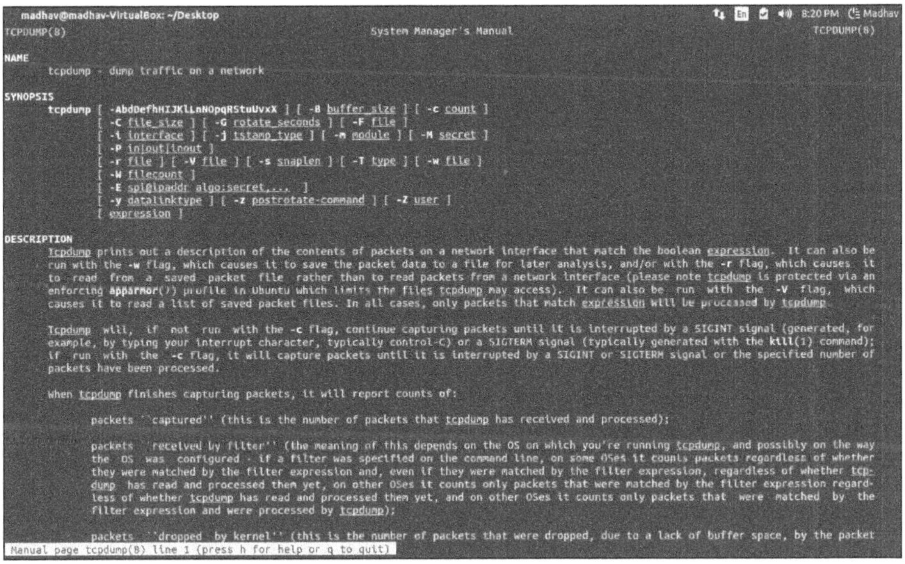

man tcpdump output

While there are a lot of options when it comes to using tcpdump, we will cover some of the important ones that are needed to capture packets.

Capturing network traffic using tcpdump

Before we begin the exercise of capturing network traffic using tcpdump, we need to understand the various sources of network traffic that we have access to on our machine.

To do this, we need to first identify the number of available interfaces on our machine. To do this we will type the following:

```
$ tcpdump -D
```

From an output perspective, we will get a list of all the available interfaces.

This will include all Ethernet, wireless, USB and FireWire interfaces. Additionally, it will offer an option — **any**, a pseudo device that will include all available interfaces:

To start capturing packets (on **eth0** by default), we need to type the following command:

```
$ tcpdump
```

This command will begin the capture process and keep going continuously until *Ctrl + C* is pressed.

All the traffic until this point on the default eth0 interface will be captured by this command.

The output will look similar to the following screenshot:

```
  madhav@madhav-VirtualBox: ~                                    ↑↓  En  🔋 (0:08) ◀) 7:59 PM  (⁞ Madhav
madhav@madhav-VirtualBox:~$ sudo tcpdump
tcpdump: verbose output suppressed, use -v or -vv for full protocol decode
listening on eth0, link-type EN10MB (Ethernet), capture size 65535 bytes
19:58:43.392947 IP 10.0.2.15.46737 > lga25s40-in-f14.1e100.net.https: Flags [.], ack 2190016478, win 59640, length 0
19:58:43.393258 IP lga25s40-in-f14.1e100.net.https > 10.0.2.15.46737: Flags [.], ack 1, win 65535, length 0
19:58:44.182725 IP 10.0.2.15.12191 > Wireless_Broadband_Router.home.domain: 47842+ PTR? 206.219.58.216.in-addr.arpa. (45)
19:58:44.198648 IP Wireless_Broadband_Router.home.domain > 10.0.2.15.12191: 47842 2/0/0 PTR lga25s40-in-f14.1e100.net., PTR lga25s40-in-f14.1e10
0.net. (90)
19:58:44.199335 IP 10.0.2.15.1870 > Wireless_Broadband_Router.home.domain: 44344+ PTR? 15.2.0.10.in-addr.arpa. (40)
19:58:44.224481 IP Wireless_Broadband_Router.home.domain > 10.0.2.15.1870: 44344 NXDomain 0/0/0 (40)
19:58:45.226625 IP 10.0.2.15.60037 > Wireless_Broadband_Router.home.domain: 53524+ PTR? 1.1.168.192.in-addr.arpa. (42)
19:58:45.231628 IP Wireless_Broadband_Router.home.domain > 10.0.2.15.60037: 53524* 1/0/0 PTR Wireless_Broadband_Router.home. (86)
19:58:45.441667 IP 10.0.2.15.59366 > yyz08s13-in-f16.1e100.net.https: Flags [.], ack 219344547, win 65535, length 0
19:58:45.441949 IP yyz08s13-in-f16.1e100.net.https > 10.0.2.15.59366: Flags [.], ack 1, win 65535, length 0
19:58:46.233797 IP 10.0.2.15.39513 > Wireless_Broadband_Router.home.domain: 29731+ PTR? 112.226.125.74.in-addr.arpa. (45)
19:58:46.248748 IP Wireless_Broadband_Router.home.domain > 10.0.2.15.39513: 29731 1/0/0 PTR yyz08s13-in-f16.1e100.net. (84)
^C
12 packets captured
12 packets received by filter
0 packets dropped by kernel
madhav@madhav-VirtualBox:~$ ▮
```

To capture packets from a different interface use the -i command-line flag. For example, the following command will capture all the packets from the **eth1** interface.

```
  madhav@madhav-VirtualBox: ~                                    ↑↓  En  🔋 (0:08) ◀) 8:02 PM  (⁞ Madhav
madhav@madhav-VirtualBox:~$ sudo tcpdump -i eth1▮
```

To write the raw data to a file use the -w command-line flag. The following command will write the first 96 bytes of every captured packet in a file called rawdata in the present directory. This can later be used for investigation purposes, as follows:

```
  madhav@madhav-VirtualBox: ~/Desktop                            ↑↓  En  🔋 (0:06) ◀) 8:10 PM  (⁞ Madhav
madhav@madhav-VirtualBox:~/Desktop$ sudo tcpdump w rawdata
tcpdump: listening on eth0, link-type EN10MB (Ethernet), capture size 65535 bytes
^C6 packets captured
6 packets received by filter
0 packets dropped by kernel
madhav@madhav-VirtualBox:~/Desktop$ ▮
```

The following screenshot depicts capturing all traffic related to a specific port (in this case port 80):

To listen to a specific port, let's say 80, we use the preceding command which captures all the packets with source or destination. To only capture packets with its source as port 80, we use `src` and for destination port as port 80, we use `dst`. Let us see the following command:

To read a trace file saved earlier using the `-w` command-line flag, use the `-r` flag in the command as shown in the following:

```
madhav@madhav-VirtualBox: ~/Desktop
madhav@madhav-VirtualBox:~/Desktop$ sudo tcpdump -r rawdata
reading from file rawdata, link-type EN10MB (Ethernet)
20:09:08.800875 IP 10.0.2.15.35772 > 199.16.156.120.https: Flags [.], ack 39621037, win 45440, length 0
20:09:08.801223 IP 199.16.156.120.https > 10.0.2.15.35772: Flags [.], ack 1, win 65535, length 0
20:09:14.153913 IP 10.0.2.15.46760 > lga25s40-in-f14.1e100.net.https: Flags [.], ack 321216690, win 31088, length 0
20:09:14.154246 IP lga25s40-in-f14.1e100.net.https > 10.0.2.15.46760: Flags [.], ack 1, win 65535, length 0
20:09:53.856905 IP 10.0.2.15.35772 > 199.16.156.120.https: Flags [.], ack 1, win 45440, length 0
20:09:53.857816 IP 199.16.156.120.https > 10.0.2.15.35772: Flags [.], ack 1, win 65535, length 0
madhav@madhav-VirtualBox:~/Desktop$
```

To capture all the packets originating from a particular source, say the host `10.0.2.15`, execute the following command:

```
madhav@madhav-VirtualBox: ~/Desktop
madhav@madhav-VirtualBox:~/Desktop$ sudo tcpdump src host 10.0.2.15 -v
```

The output derived would be as follows:

```
madhav@madhav-VirtualBox: ~/Desktop
madhav@madhav-VirtualBox:~/Desktop$ sudo tcpdump src host 10.0.2.15 -v
tcpdump: listening on eth0, link-type EN10MB (Ethernet), capture size 65535 bytes
20:27:49.598158 IP (tos 0x0, ttl 64, id 6432, offset 0, flags [DF], proto UDP (17), length 65)
    10.0.2.15.21661 > Wireless_Broadband_Router.home.domain: 61651+ A? clients2.google.com. (37)
20:27:49.617663 IP (tos 0x0, ttl 64, id 51460, offset 0, flags [DF], proto TCP (6), length 60)
    10.0.2.15.46820 > lga25s40-in-f14.1e100.net.https: Flags [S], cksum 0xc046 (incorrect -> 0xf862), seq 926118472, win 29200, options [mss 146
0,sackOK,TS val 899916 ecr 0,nop,wscale 7], length 0
20:27:49.629511 IP (tos 0x0, ttl 64, id 51461, offset 0, flags [DF], proto TCP (6), length 40)
    10.0.2.15.46820 > lga25s40-in-f14.1e100.net.https: Flags [.], cksum 0xc032 (incorrect -> 0x5fa9), ack 467968002, win 29200, length 0
20:27:49.630276 IP (tos 0x0, ttl 64, id 51462, offset 0, flags [DF], proto TCP (6), length 557)
    10.0.2.15.46820 > lga25s40-in-f14.1e100.net.https: Flags [P.], cksum 0xc237 (incorrect -> 0xab69), seq 0:517, ack 1, win 29200, length 517
20:27:49.648450 IP (tos 0x0, ttl 64, id 51463, offset 0, flags [DF], proto TCP (6), length 40)
    10.0.2.15.46820 > lga25s40-in-f14.1e100.net.https: Flags [.], cksum 0xc032 (incorrect -> 0x59df), ack 150, win 30016, length 0
20:27:49.649443 IP (tos 0x0, ttl 64, id 51464, offset 0, flags [DF], proto TCP (6), length 91)
    10.0.2.15.46820 > lga25s40-in-f14.1e100.net.https: Flags [P.], cksum 0xc065 (incorrect -> 0xe06c), seq 517:568, ack 150, win 30016, length 5
1
20:27:49.650458 IP (tos 0x0, ttl 64, id 51465, offset 0, flags [DF], proto TCP (6), length 93)
    10.0.2.15.46820 > lga25s40-in-f14.1e100.net.https: Flags [P.], cksum 0xc067 (incorrect -> 0xcedc), seq 568:621, ack 150, win 30016, length 5
3
20:27:49.650964 IP (tos 0x0, ttl 64, id 51466, offset 0, flags [DF], proto TCP (6), length 90)
    10.0.2.15.46820 > lga25s40-in-f14.1e100.net.https: Flags [P.], cksum 0xc064 (incorrect -> 0xd7a7), seq 621:671, ack 150, win 30016, length 5
0
20:27:49.651679 IP (tos 0x0, ttl 64, id 51467, offset 0, flags [DF], proto TCP (6), length 82)
    10.0.2.15.46820 > lga25s40-in-f14.1e100.net.https: Flags [P.], cksum 0xc05c (incorrect -> 0x4276), seq 671:713, ack 150, win 30016, length 4
2
20:27:49.652389 IP (tos 0x0, ttl 64, id 51468, offset 0, flags [DF], proto TCP (6), length 250)
    10.0.2.15.46820 > lga25s40-in-f14.1e100.net.https: Flags [P.], cksum 0xc104 (incorrect -> 0x9518), seq 713:923, ack 150, win 30016, length 2
10
20:27:49.652978 IP (tos 0x0, ttl 64, id 51469, offset 0, flags [DF], proto TCP (6), length 771)
    10.0.2.15.46820 > lga25s40-in-f14.1e100.net.https: Flags [P.], cksum 0xc38d (incorrect -> 0xc949), seq 923:1654, ack 150, win 30016, length
731
20:27:49.659940 IP (tos 0x0, ttl 64, id 51470, offset 0, flags [DF], proto TCP (6), length 40)
    10.0.2.15.46820 > lga25s40-in-f14.1e100.net.https: Flags [.], cksum 0xc032 (incorrect -> 0x558c), ack 248, win 30016, length 0
20:27:49.661086 IP (tos 0x0, ttl 64, id 51471, offset 0, flags [DF], proto TCP (6), length 78)
    10.0.2.15.46820 > lga25s40-in-f14.1e100.net.https: Flags [P.], cksum 0xc058 (incorrect -> 0xcfb5), seq 1654:1692, ack 248, win 30016, length
38
20:27:49.698816 IP (tos 0x0, ttl 64, id 51472, offset 0, flags [DF], proto TCP (6), length 40)
    10.0.2.15.46820 > lga25s40-in-f14.1e100.net.https: Flags [.], cksum 0xc032 (incorrect -> 0x4fd3), ack 475, win 31088, length 0
20:27:49.700479 IP (tos 0x0, ttl 64, id 51473, offset 0, flags [DF], proto TCP (6), length 40)
```

Tcpdump supports the usage of logical arguments such as AND and OR, they can be used as shown in the following; however, the argument being passed to tcpdump must be in the form of a Boolean expression. To capture all the packets originating from a particular source, say the host `10.0.2.15` and destination port 80, execute the command as shown in the following screenshot:

The output derived will be as shown in the following screenshot:

This brief tutorial on capturing traffic using tcpdump acts as a primer on the path to network forensics.

Collecting network traffic using Wireshark

While tcpdump is a cool tool to capture network traffic, Wireshark is widely used when it comes to network forensic investigations. In this section, we will focus on installing and using Wireshark to capture network traffic.

Wireshark is available for most of the OS, including Windows, Mac OS, and most flavors of Linux.

It is available for free download at `https://www.wireshark.org/download.html`.

Using Wireshark

Install Wireshark using the **Ubuntu Software Center**, as shown in the following screenshot:

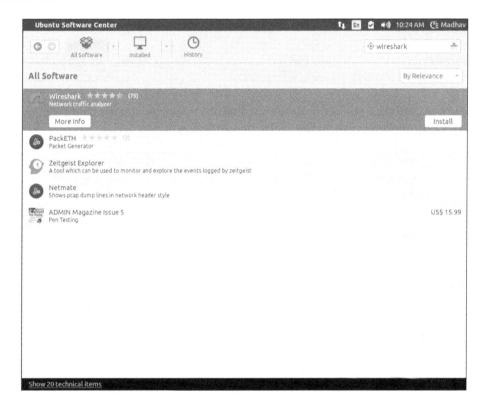

Run Wireshark with network privileges either directly or using the terminal to start capturing packets, as shown in the following screenshot:

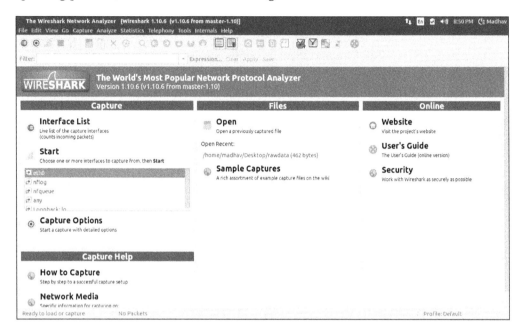

Configure according to network topology and other specific details using the **Capture Options**, as shown in the following screenshot:

To get started, all we need to do is select an interface to start capturing packets from. Let's select eth0, as follows:

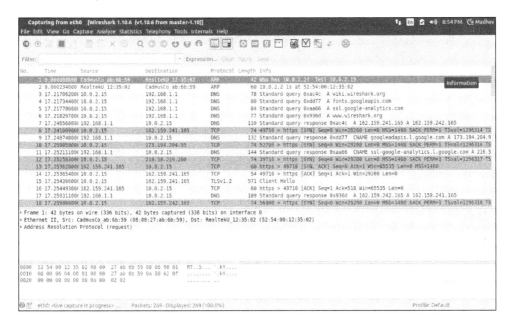

When we select an interface to start capturing packets (eth0), the output is as shown in the following screenshot:

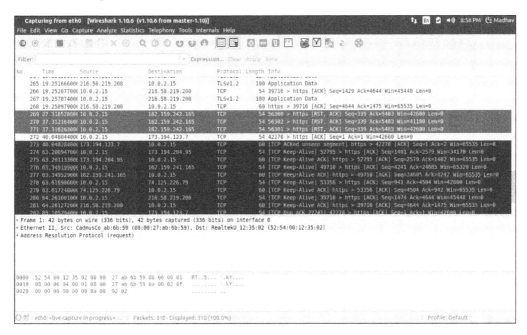

To save the raw data in a file, click on the save to file button and choose the required directory, as shown in the following screenshot:

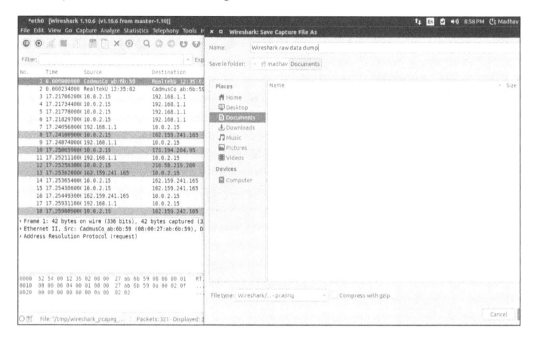

That's it! Nice and easy. In the future chapters, we will analyze the captured data.

Collecting network logs

All machines on your network are not likely to be Linux; therefore, to keep a balance of things, we will use Windows as an example for this exercise.

To start **Event Viewer**, click on the start button and write `Event Viewer`, as shown in the following screenshot:

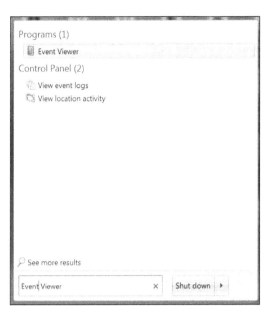

The Event Viewer will open up as shown in the following screenshot:

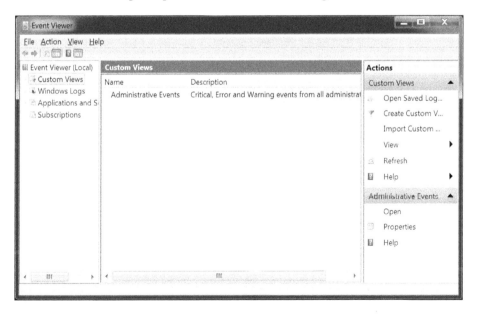

Event Viewer stores consists of the following components:

- **Custom Views**
- **Windows Logs**
- **Applications and Services Logs**

The different views stores are as follows:

- **Custom Views**:
  - ○ **Administrative Events**: This contains the **Critical**, **Error**, and **Warning** events from all administrative logs, as shown in the following screenshot:

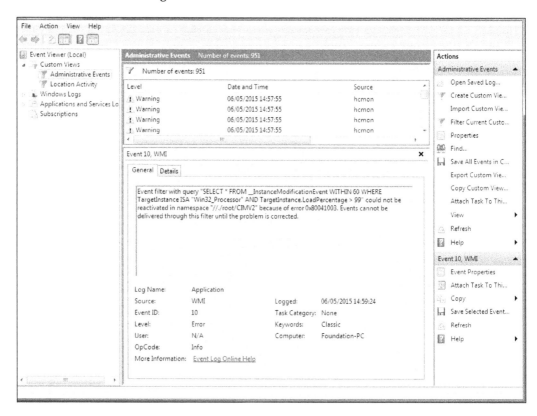

- ° **Location Activity**: As the name suggests, this contains the location activity, as shown in the following screenshot:

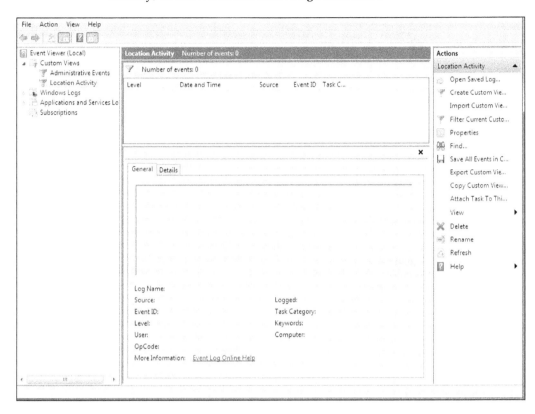

- • **Windows Logs**: Windows log stores events from legacy applications and events that apply to the entire system:

- ○ **Application**: The **Application** log stores events logged by the applications or programs. For example, a database *progmemory* might record a file error in the application log. The developers of the *progmemory* module decide which events to log, as shown in the following screenshot:

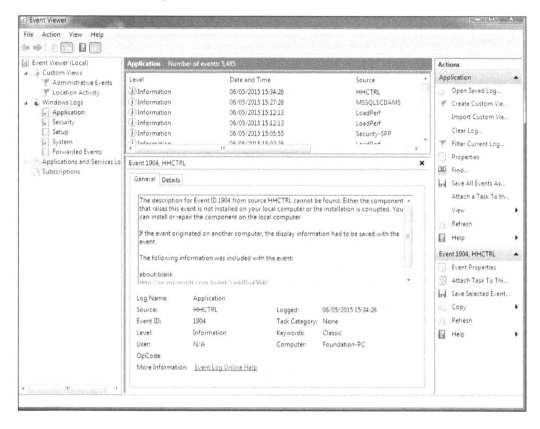

- ○ **Security**: The **Security** log stores events such as valid and invalid log on attempts as well as events related to resource use, such as creating, opening, or deleting files or other objects. Administrators can specify which events are recorded in the security log. For example, if you have enabled logon auditing, attempts to log on to the system are recorded in the security log, as shown in the following screenshot:

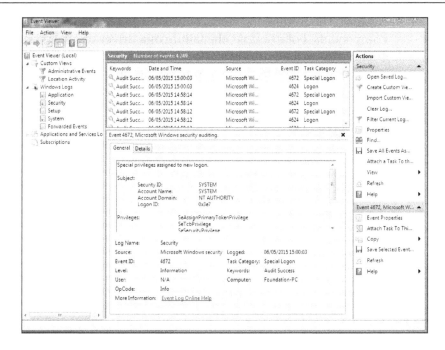

° **Setup**: The **Setup** log stores events related to application set up, as shown in the following screenshot:

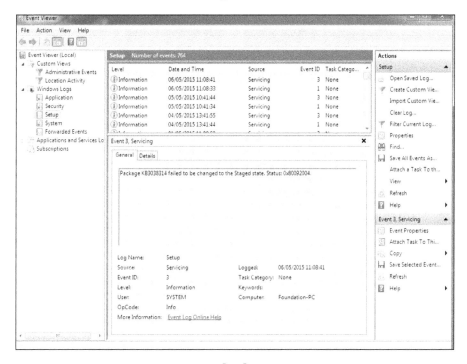

○ **System**: The **System** log stores events logged by the Windows system components. For example, the failure of a driver or other system component to load during startup is recorded in the **System** log. The event types logged by system components are predetermined by Windows, as shown in the following screenshot:

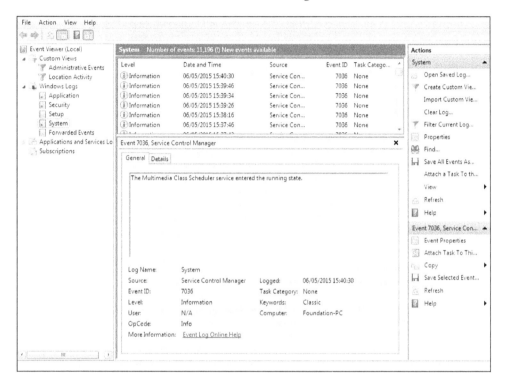

○ **Forwarded Events**: The **Forwarded Events** logs store events collected from remote computers, as shown in the following screenshot:

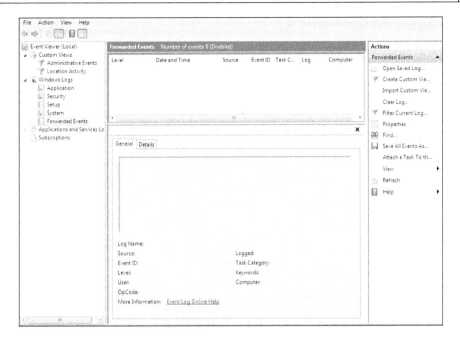

- **Application and Services Logs**: These logs store events from a single application or component rather than events that might have system-wide impact:

    ○ **Broadband Wireless LAN**:

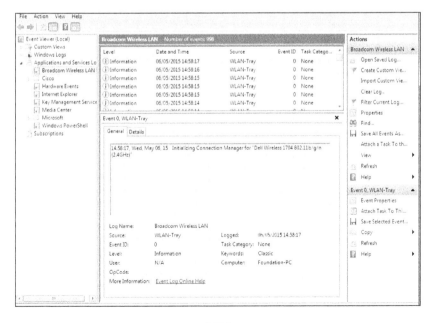

○ **Hardware Events:**

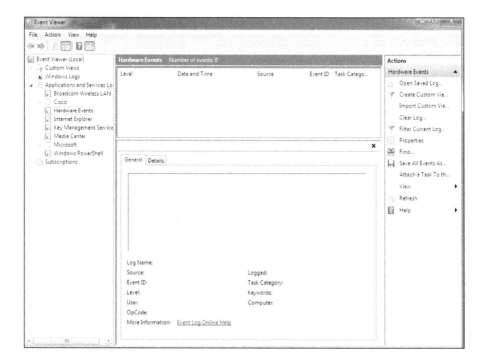

○ **Internet Explorer:**

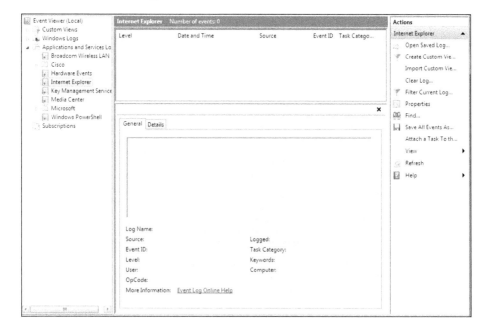

○ **Key Management Services**:

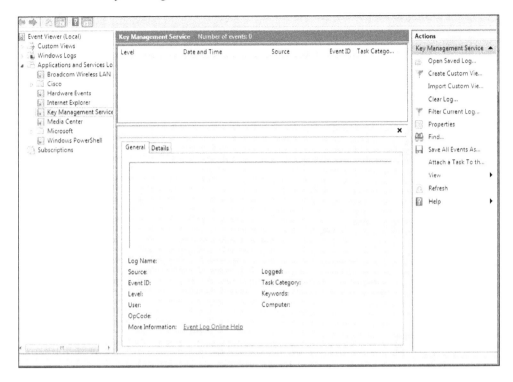

○ **Media Center**:

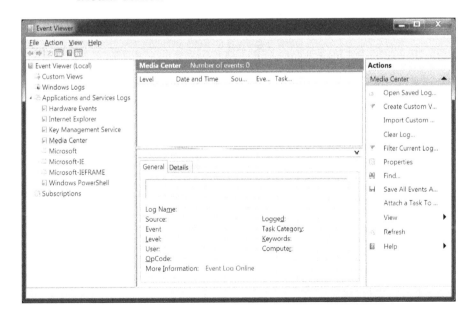

○ Windows event logs:

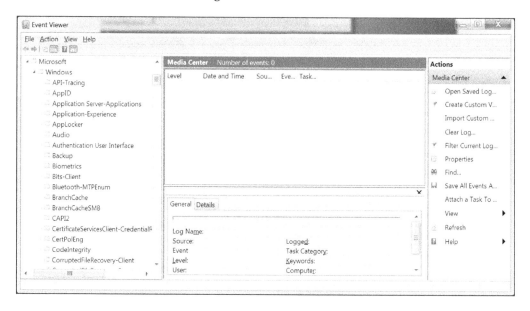

Acquiring memory using FTK Imager

Memory is a very important source of evidence in an investigation process. All activities that happen on a system are usually reflected in the memory at the time.

The following is a step-by-step guide to acquire a system's volatile memory using the product **FTK Imager**.

This can be downloaded for free at `http://accessdata.com/product-download`.

1. Run FTK Imager as an administrator, as shown in the following screenshot:

2. Click on the **File** menu and select **Capture Memory**, as shown in the following screenshot:

3. Browse the destination folder, where you want to save the acquired memory dump, as shown in the following screenshot:

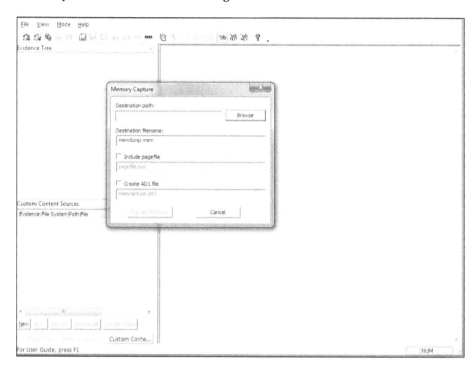

4. Click on **Browse** and create a destination folder, as shown in the following screenshot:

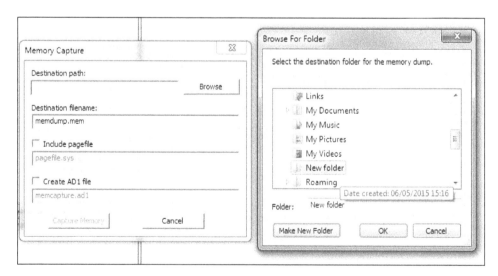

5. After creating the destination folder, click on **Capture Memory**, as shown in the following screenshot:

6. Click on **Capture Memory** and the memory dumping will start, as shown in the following screenshot:

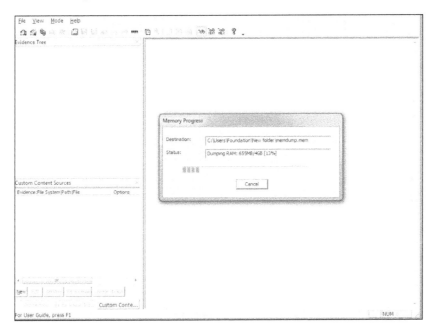

7. Creation of pagefile starts after the completion of memory dump, as shown in the following screenshot:

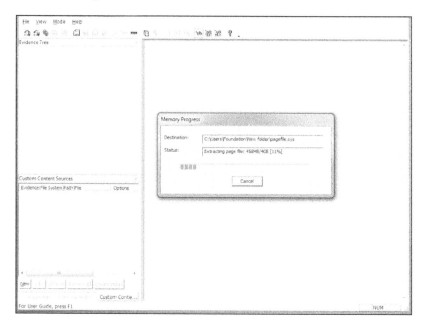

8. Creation of the AD1 file starts after the completion of pagefile (logical containers), as shown in the following screenshot:

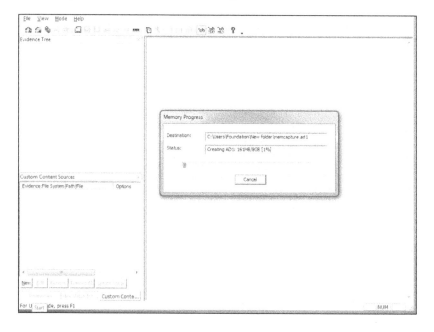

9. Once the acquisition is completed, click on the **Close** button, as shown in the following screenshot:

We are now done.

Summary

In this chapter, you learned how to acquire evidence from different sources. You were also exposed to a number of tools such as tcpdump, Wireshark, Event Viewer, and FTK Imager. We have also studied how to use these tools to acquire evidence that could be relevant to our case.

The next chapter moves us along our journey of acquiring knowledge and skills in the network forensics arena. You will learn how to intercept and analyze network traffic using a number of tools. We will also get an opportunity to look at a case study, where we will see how this knowledge has been put into practice in the real world.

3

Capturing & Analyzing
Data Packets

"Unless you capture the moment, it's gone!"

– Samir Datt

In this chapter, you will learn to get your hands dirty by actually capturing and analyzing network traffic. We will start by understanding the network configuration that is required to capture data packets, including the concept of port mirroring, and then go on to using different software tools to capture and analyze network traffic with real-world scenarios of accessing data over the Internet and the resultant network capture.

The chapter will cover the following topics:

- Tapping into network traffic
- Packet sniffing and analysis using Wireshark
- Packet sniffing and analysis using NetworkMiner
- Case study – sniffing out an insider

Tapping into network traffic

As a network 007, our objective of gathering evidence can only be met if we dive into the data packets that flow across the network. To do this, we need to enhance our understanding of networks and the technology behind hubs and switches on the network.

In early networks, computers connected to each other via co-axial cables, followed by a switchover to the star topology and the use of Ethernet hubs. The following diagram shows a basic co-axial network:

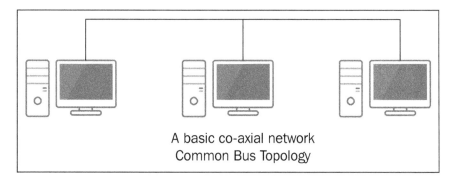

A basic co-axial network
Common Bus Topology

The bus topology gave way to the star topology, as depicted in the following diagram:

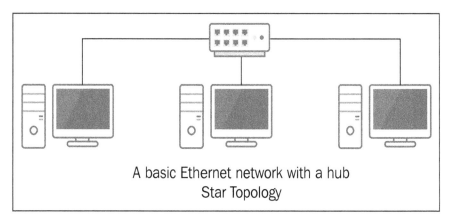

A basic Ethernet network with a hub
Star Topology

In such a case, all the network traffic is broadcast to each and every node on the network and it is expected that the correct node will collect the traffic that is meant for it. In such a situation, if any **network interface card** (**NIC**) is in the *promiscuous mode*, it is able to capture any traffic that is meant for other nodes on the network. Software network sniffing tools, such as Wireshark, will automatically put the network card in the promiscuous mode to capture the data packets that travel on the network.

Passive and active sniffing on networks

Today, enterprises deploy numerous switching devices on the network that divide the traffic into multiple segments. A number of these enterprise switches come with additional port(s) called **Switched Port Analyzer** (**SPAN**) ports. This is also known as a mirror port. This works in active mode. This means that it is the job of the network device to physically copy the network packets to the mirror port.

This SPAN port is designed to copy traffic (both RX and TX), which can then be analyzed by an analysis device that is attached to the network. To understand this better, we need to realize that the networks that operate at 100 Mbits or better are full duplex networks. This means that the actual maximum data flowing through a 100 Mbit connection is actually 200 Mbit (2 x 100 MBit) — 100 Mbit for each direction. Thus, a network sniffing device has to cope with the traffic and copy it to the network mirror port for successful packet capturing. Now, for a device rated with 100 MBit capacity, it will only be able to handle a full duplex setup if the data traffic is at 50% capacity — what this means is that if the simultaneous data transmitted and the data received equals 100 Mbit, the mirror port will be able to handle it. Anything greater than this will result in packet losses.

In addition to this, the *active* aspect of this requires CPU resources. This may affect or overload the network switch, causing it to underperform its main functions.

The other alternative to the SPAN or mirror port is the network tap. A **test access point** (**TAP**) performs packet sniffing in passive mode. In such a case, network packets are copied on to the TAP ports. Usually, there are separate TAP ports for traffic from each direction, that is, a different port for TX and a different one for RX. This ensures that complete network traffic is captured.

The following diagram depicts a TAP deployed between a network switch and Internet to capture both incoming and outgoing packets:

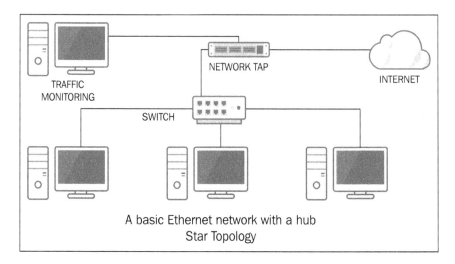

Both of these have different inherent advantages and disadvantages, as enumerated in the following table:

Feature	TAP	SPAN
Price	Expensive	Economical
Additional Hardware	Required	Not required
Operational Mode	Passive	Active with additional burden on device CPU
Separate Channels for RX & TX	Yes	No
Packet Loss	None	Yes – when traffic exceeds port capacity (network saturation greater than 50%)
Captures Intra switch traffic	No	Yes

Packet sniffing and analysis using Wireshark

In the previous chapter, we discussed how to install Wireshark on our computers.

Let's take a quick look at the Wireshark interface:

As we can see, the interface is quite intuitive. Once a few basic decisions, as outlined in the previous chapter (such as the selection of interface to capture from) have been made, the capture operation is initiated.

Once the capture operation begins, the interface looks similar to the following screenshot:

Packet List pane

Each row in the preceding screenshot represents a packet captured by Wireshark.

When one of the rows/packets is highlighted and right-clicked, we can see the TCP stream for the in-depth detail about its contents, as shown in the following screenshot:

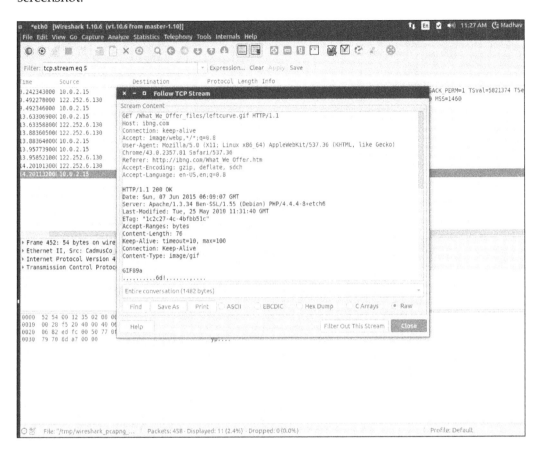

Another cool thing that you can get Wireshark to do is to resolve the IP addresses to real-world human-readable domains using **Address Resolution**, as shown in the following screenshot:

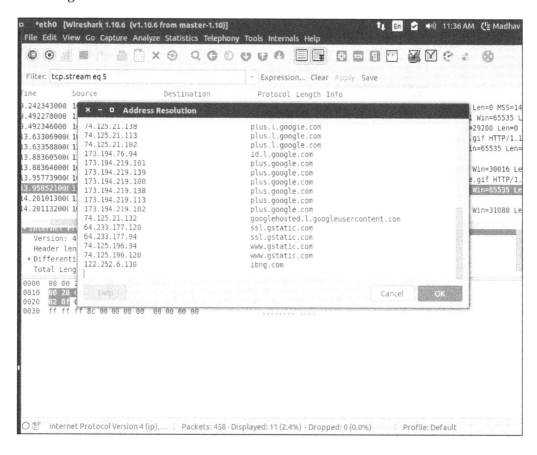

The Wireshark main window is broadly divided into three distinct areas or *panes*, as follows:

- The top-most pane is called the **Packet List** pane
- The middle pane is called the **Packet Details** pane
- The bottom-most pane is called the **Packet Bytes** pane

All these names are self-explanatory.

When we look at the top-most pane, we can see a list of the packets captured by Wireshark, as shown in the following:

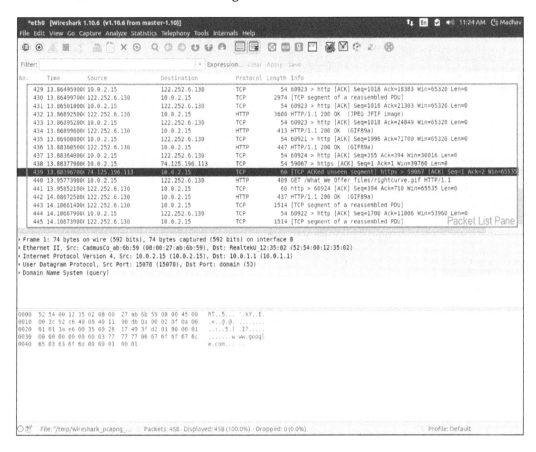

This lists out the packet number, time of capture, source and destination IP address, protocol, length, and associated information, as shown in the following:

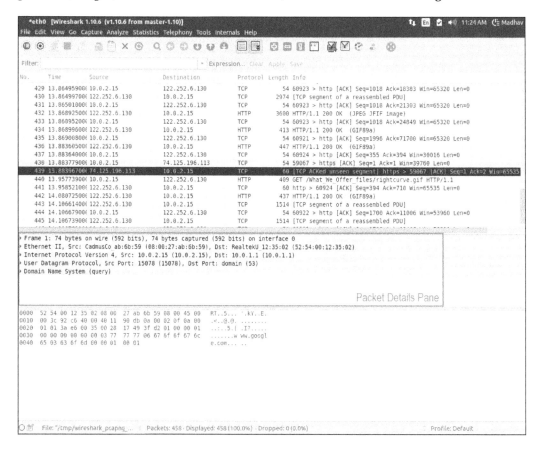

Whenever a specific packet is highlighted in the top-most pane, its details get listed in the Packet Details pane.

From a deep-dive perspective, this allows us to gain a deeper insight in the metadata related to the packet being inspected.

The metadata that is shown actually consists of the protocols and the protocol fields of the selected packet. These are presented in a tree structure that can be expanded or collapsed by the user.

Some protocol fields that are displayed include generated fields and links. The generated fields are the information that is generated by Wireshark and are usually displayed in brackets. This information is actually derived from the context and content of other related packets in the capture file. Links are usually generated if Wireshark detects a relationship with another packet in the capture file. Just like any hyperlinks, these are underlined and colored in blue. If double-clicked, the user jumps to that specific packet.

The third pane is the Packet Bytes pane. Whenever we highlight a specific packet in the Packet List pane, its contents are visible in the **hex dump** format. This is visible in the following screenshot:

The left-most column denotes the offset, the next portion is the hex, and the last portion is the contents of the packet in ASCII. As we can see, in this case, the website being accessed is `www.google.com`.

A quick look at the Packet List pane shows us that different packets are colored differently as shown in the following screenshot:

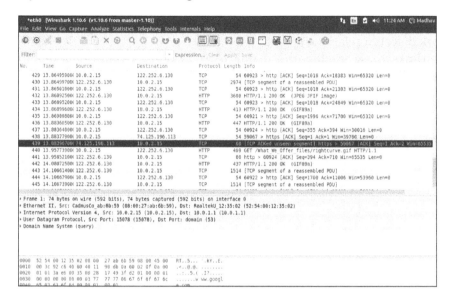

Wireshark has a complex coloring scheme when it comes to packets.

This is shown in the following image:

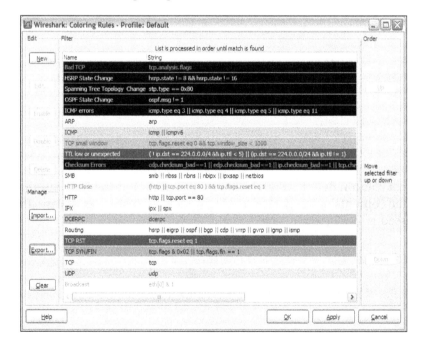

Wireshark has a number of valuable features when it comes to the analysis of captured packets.

No criminal or wrongdoer wants to be caught. They constantly devise new ways to prevent detection. Due to the increasing use of simple employee monitoring software in organizations, we have suspects using **Voice over IP** (**VoIP**) for communication with their accomplices.

One of the really useful features of Wireshark in such a scenario is in the ability to capture and analyze VoIP traffic. We can use the **Telephony | VoIP Calls** option to decode the VoIP packets and play back live conversations. That's the real 007 in action!!! This can be seen in the following screenshot:

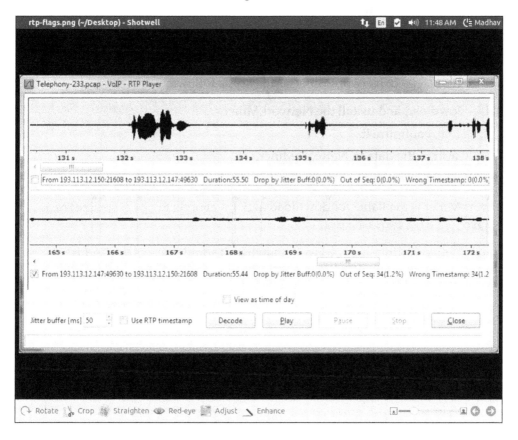

The best way to learn using Wireshark is to follow the instructions provided in the previous chapter as well as this one and get started with hands-on capturing and analysis of traffic on your network. Remember to take permissions first—you may quickly find that sniffing networks can actually reveal a lot of confidential data.

Packet sniffing and analysis using NetworkMiner

NetworkMiner is a passive network sniffing or network forensic tool. It is called a passive tool as it does not send out requests—it sits silently on the network, capturing every packet in the promiscuous mode.

NetworkMiner is host-centric. This means that it will classify data based on hosts rather than packets, which is what most sniffers such as Wireshark do.

The different steps to NetworkMiner usage are as follows:

1. Download and install the NetworkMiner.
2. Then, configure it.
3. Capture the data in NetworkMiner.
4. Finally, analyze the data.

NetworkMiner is available for download at SourceForge: `http://sourceforge.net/projects/networkminer/`.

Though NetworkMiner is not as well known as it should be, it's host-centric approach is refreshingly different and effective. Allowing the users to classify traffic based on the IP addresses and not packets helps us to zero in on activities related to the specific computers that are under suspicion or are being investigated.

The NetworkMiner interface is shown in the following screenshot:

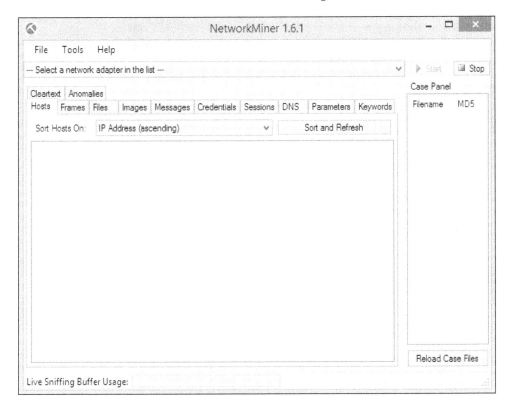

To begin using NetworkMiner, we start by selecting a network adapter from the drop-down list. NetworkMiner places this adapter in the promiscuous mode. Clicking **Start** begins NetworkMiner on the task of packet collection.

While NetworkMiner has the capability of collecting data packets across the network, its real strength comes in to play after the data has been collected. In most of the scenarios, it makes more sense to use Wireshark to capture packets and then use NetworkMiner to do the analysis on the .pcap file that is captured.

As soon as data capturing begins, NetworkMiner swings into action by sorting the packets based on the host IP addresses. This is extremely useful since it allows us to identify traffic that is specific to a single IP on the network. Consider that we have a single suspect with a known IP on the network, then we can focus our investigative resources on just that single IP address.

Some really great additional features include the ability to identify the **media access control** (**MAC**) address of the **network interface card** (**NIC**) in use and also the OS of the suspect system. In fact, the icon on the left-hand side of the IP address shows the OS icon, if detected, as shown in the following screenshot:

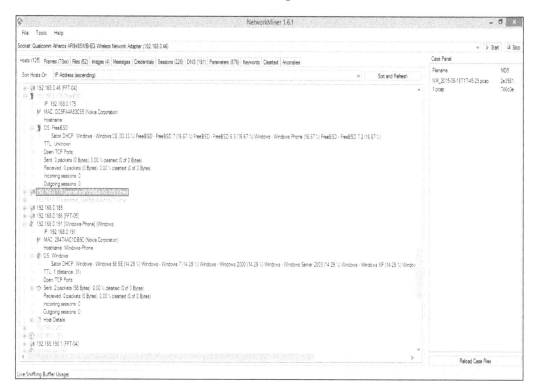

As we can see in the preceding image, some of the devices that are connected to the network under investigation are Windows and BSD devices.

The next tab is the **Frames** tab. The **Frames** tab view is similar to that of Wireshark and is perhaps one of the lesser used tabs in NetworkMiner, due to the fact that there are so many other richer options available, as shown in the following screenshot:

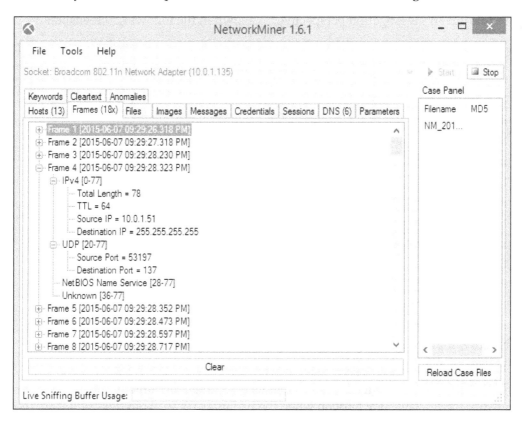

It gives us inputs on the packet length, source and destination IP address, as well as **Time to Live** (**TTL**) of the packet.

NetworkMiner has the ability to collate the packets and then reconstruct the constituent files for viewing by the investigator. These files are shown in the **Files** tab.

Assuming that some files were copied/accessed over a network share, it would be possible to view the reconstructed file in the **Files** tab.

The **Files** tab also depicts the SSL certificates used over a network. This can also be useful from an investigation perspective, as shown in the following screenshot:

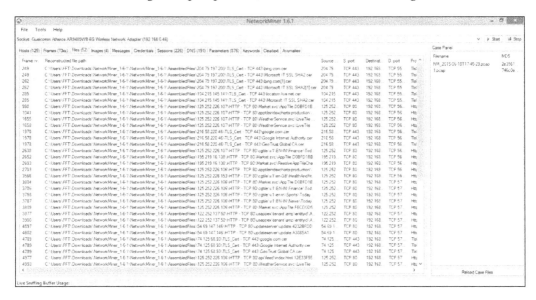

Similarly, if pictures have been viewed over the network, these are reconstructed in the **Images** tab.

In fact, this can be quite useful especially, when scanned documents are a part of the network traffic. This may happen when the bad guys try to avoid detection from the keyword-based searching.

The following is an image depicting the **Images** tab:

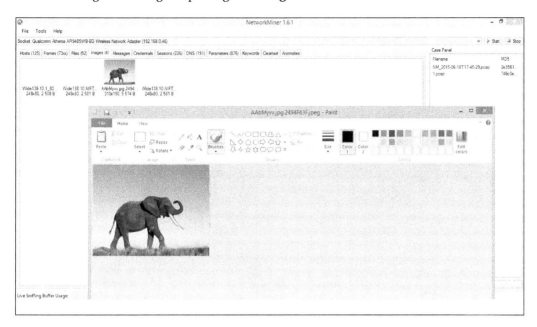

The reconstructed graphics are usually depicted as thumbnails. Right-clicking the thumbnail allows us to open the graphic in a picture editor/viewer.

DNS queries are also accessible via the **DNS** tab, as shown in the following image:

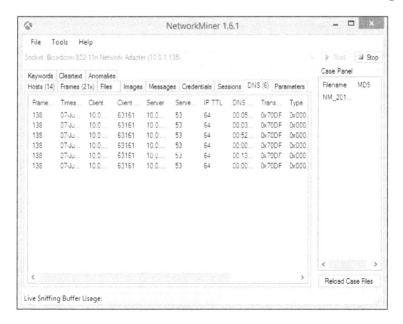

There are additional tabs available that are notable from the perspective of an investigation.

One of these is the **Credentials** tab.

This stores the information related to interactions involving the exchange of credentials with resources that require logons. It is not uncommon to find usernames and passwords for plain-text logons listed under this tab. One can also find user accounts for popular sites such as Gmail and Facebook.

A screenshot of the **Credentials** tab is as follows:

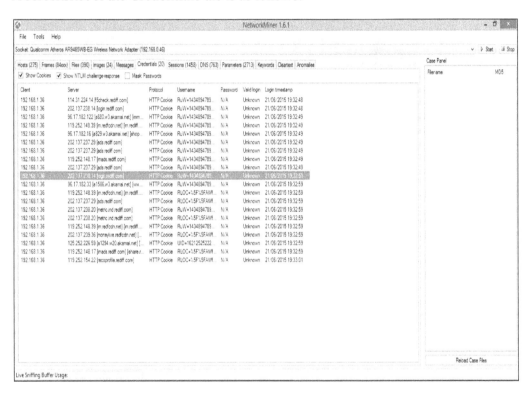

In a number of cases, it is possible to determine the usernames and passwords of certain websites.

Another great feature in NetworkMiner is the ability to import a set of keywords that are to be used to search within packets in the captured `.pcap` file.

This allows us to separate packets that contain our keywords of interest.

The following screenshot shows the **Keywords** tab with the option to search for specific keywords:

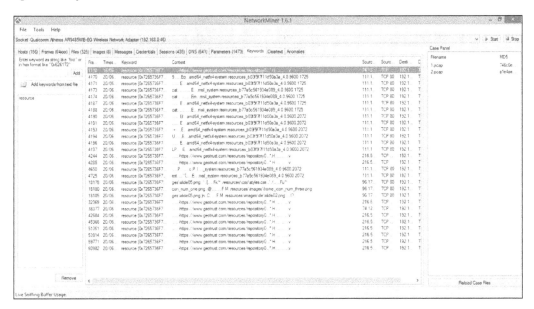

Case study – tracking down an insider

XYZ Corporation, a medium-sized Government contractor, found that it had begun to lose business to a tiny competitor that seemed to know exactly what the sales team at XYZ Corp was planning.

The senior management suspected that an insider was leaking information to the competitor.

A network forensic 007 was called in to investigate the problem.

A preliminary information-gathering exercise was initiated and a list of keywords was compiled to help in identifying packets that contained information of interest. A list of possible suspects, who had access to the confidential information, was also compiled.

The specific network segment relating to the department in question was put under network surveillance. Wireshark was deployed to capture all the network traffic. Additional storage was made available to store the .pcap files generated by Wireshark.

The collected .pcap files were analyzed using NetworkMiner.

The following screenshot depicts Wireshark capturing traffic:

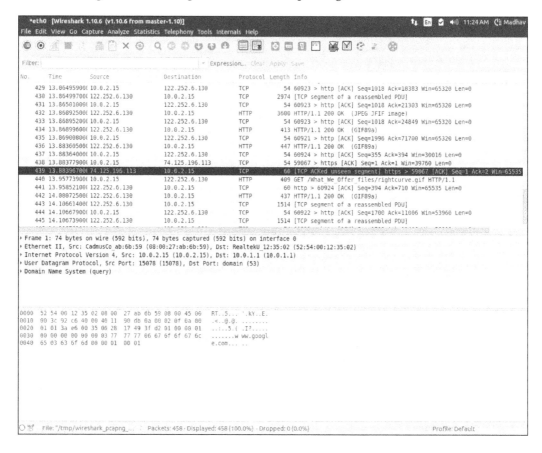

An in-depth analysis of network traffic produced the following findings:

- An image showing the registration certificate of the company that was competing with XYZ Corp, providing the names of the directors

- The address of the company in the registration certificate was the residential address of the sales manager of XYZ Corp

- E-mail communications using personal e-mail addresses between the directors of the competing company and the senior manager sales of XYZ Corp

- Further offline analysis showed that the sales manager's wife was related to the director of the competing company

- It was also seen that the sales manager was connecting to the office Wi-Fi network using his Android phone

- The sales manager was noted to be accessing cloud storage using his phone and transferring important files and contact lists

- It was noted that the sales manager was also in close communication with a female employee in the accounts department and that the connection was *intimate*

The information collected so far was very indicative of the sales manager's involvement with competitors.

Based on the preceding network forensics exercise, it was recommended that a full-fledged digital forensic exercise should be initiated, including that of his assigned laptop and phone device. It was also recommended that sufficient corroborating evidence should be collected using log analysis, RAM analysis, and disk forensics to initiate legal/breach of trust action against the suspect(s).

Summary

In this chapter, we moved our skills up a notch. We learned how to analyze the captured packets to see what is happening on the network. We also studied how to see the traffic from the specific IP addresses as well as protocol-specific traffic. We also understood how to look for specific traffic based on keywords. Files, private credentials, and images have been examined to identify activities of interest. We have now become a lot better at investigating network activity.

In the next chapter, we are going to expand our skills and further our understanding of wireless networks, their security, as well as the common attacks that are out there. We will also look at how to sniff traffic and analyze it from our perspective.

4
Going Wireless

"Freedom always comes at a price"

– Samir Datt

Today, people desire to be free from the restraining and restricting wires. Always connected and always online, the growth of this desire has fueled the proliferation of wireless networks. Who doesn't have Wi-Fi at home or at their place of work? Our phones are connected using Wi-Fi, our tablets are connected over Wi-Fi and with the advent of the **Internet of Things** (**IoT**), even our household devices are connected over Wi-Fi or will be in the future!

However, the freedom of a wireless existence comes at a price. Wireless networks broadcast a signal that is open to the air. With no physical limitations except those of range, this signal is open to interception and interpretation by the bad guys.

In the previous chapters, we saw how information travels in packets over the network physical layer. In wireless LAN networks, the data packets are broadcast wirelessly over the air. The receiving device reads the packet header, identifies the packets that are meant for it, and collects just those while discarding the rest. This means that any network device that is on the wireless network can receive the data packets meant for somebody else if it is set up and configured to do so.

To enhance your understanding of the wireless world and upgrade the ability to investigate it, we will cover the following topics in this chapter:

- Laying the foundation – IEEE 802.11
- Understanding wireless protection and security
- Discussing common attacks on Wi-Fi networks
- Capturing and analyzing wireless traffic

Laying the foundation – IEEE 802.11

At the **Institute of Electrical and Electronics Engineers (IEEE)**, a working group was set up to create specifications for **wireless local area networks (WLANs)**. This slowly evolved into a family of specifications known as the IEEE 802.11 specifications for wireless LANs.

The Ethernet protocol forms the foundation of all the 802.11 specifications.

As investigators who are getting ready to explore the forensics of wireless networks, it is important to develop an understanding of the underlying technology. The 802.11 specifications allow us to gain an insight into data speeds, spectrums, encoding, and so on.

These standards are downloadable and available free of charge from the IEEE website at `http://standards.ieee.org/about/get/802/802.11.html`.

In a nutshell, the 802.11 specifications are a set of **media access control (MAC)** and **physical layer (PHY)** specifications that govern communications in wireless LANs in the 2.4, 3.6. 6, and 60 GHz frequency bands.

The 802.11 specifications were first released in 1997. These consisted of a series of half-duplex, over-the-air modulation techniques that use the same basic protocol. Since then, they have undergone considerable changes and a number of specifications have been released. Amendments have also been added to the specifications in order to address further evolution. In fact, all wireless network products adhere to one or the other 802.11 specifications and amendments.

There are several specifications in the 802.11 family, as shown in the following:

- 802.11: The 802.11 specification was the first wireless LAN specification released in 1997 and it allowed transmissions in the 1 or 2 Mbps (Megabits per second) range. This happened in the 2.4 GHz band using either **Frequency Hopping Spread Spectrum (FHSS)** or **Direct Sequence Spread Spectrum (DSSS)**.

- 802.11a: The 802.11a specification was designed as an extension to the 802.11 specifications. This applied to wireless LANs in the 5 GHz range and provided speeds up to 54 Mbps. This did not use the FHSS or DSSS; however, it used an **Orthogonal frequency-division multiplexing (OFDM)** scheme. This offers at least 23 non-overlapping channels for communications.

- 802.11b: The 802.11b specification was the most popular of the early specifications. This was released in 1999 and allowed wireless functionality that was comparable to Ethernet. This was also referred to as the 802.11 High Rate or 802.11 Wi-Fi. This used the 2.4 GHz frequency band and allowed 11 Mbps transmission with a fallback to 5.5, 2, and 1 Mbps speed. This specification only uses DSSS. Due to this choice of the 2.4 GHz frequency band, 802.11b equipment can occasionally suffer interference from microwaves, cordless telephones, and Bluetooth devices, which also share the same frequency band under the US **Federal Communications Commission (FCC)** rules.

- 802.11e: The 802.11e specification is a draft standard that is an enhancement of the 802.11a and 802.11b specifications. It adds **Quality of Service (QoS)** features and multimedia support for wireless LANs as per the previous standards. It maintains full backward compatibility.

- 802.11g: Another popular specification that was widely adopted by WLAN device manufacturers and users is the 802.11g. It is used for transmissions over short distances at speeds up to 54 Mbps in 2.4 GHz bands. Just like the 802.11b, this can also suffer interference from microwave ovens, cordless phones, Bluetooth devices, and so on.

- 802.11n: The 802.11n specification enhances the previous 802.11 standards by adding **multiple input, multiple output (MIMO)**. In this case, additional transmitter and receiver antennas allow increased data throughput and range. Real speed is up to four or five times faster than 100 Mbits and can reach up to 250 Mbits at the PHY level.

- 802.11ac: This builds upon the previous standards to deliver data speeds of 433 Mbps per spatial stream or 1.3 Gbps in a three-antenna design. This works in the 5 Ghz range and supports higher bandwidth for higher wireless speeds.

- 802.11ac Wave 2: This specification is the same as the previous specification, except that this uses MIMO technology and other enhancements to theoretically increase throughput to nearly 7 Gbps (6.93 Gbps, actually).

- 802.11ad: This specification is under development and will operate in the 60 GHz band. The expected theoretical data transfer rate is expected to be up to 7 Gigabits per second.

- 802.11r: This specification supports VoIP roaming and handoff over multiple access points on a Wi-Fi network with the 802.1X authentication.

- 802.1X: This is different from the 802.11x family of specifications. The IEEE 802.1X standard is designed for port-based **Network Access Control (NAC)** to restrict the use and enable secure communications between authenticated/authorized devices.

All the major 802.11 specifications can be represented in an easy-to-understand table, as shown in the following:

802.11 Standard	Year of Release	Frequency Band GHz	Modulation	Data Transmission Rate (Mbits/sec)
802.11	1997	2.4 GHz	DSSS/FHSS	2 Mbit/s
802.11a	1999	5 GHz	OFDM	54 Mbit/s
802.11 ac	2013	5 GHz	OFDM	6.93 Gbit/s
802.11ad	2012	60 GHz	SC-OFDM	6.76 Gbit/s
802.11b	1999	2.4 GHz	DSSS	11 Mbit/s
802.11g	2003	2.4 GHz	DSSS/OFDM	54 Mbit/s
802.11n	2009	2.4/5 GHz	OFDM	600 Mbit/s

Full form of abbreviations used in the table are as follows:

- **DSSS**: Direct Sequence Spread Spectrum
- **FHSS**: Frequency Hopping Spread Spectrum
- **OFDM**: Orthogonal frequency-division multiplexing
- **SC-OFDM**: Single Carrier-Orthogonal frequency division multiplex

Now that we have developed an understanding of what is going on at the MAC and physical layers, let's move on to understanding a bit about wireless protection and security.

Understanding wireless protection and security

Before we move onto forensic investigation of wireless security breaches, we need to understand the various facets of wireless protection and the elements of security therein.

Let's start with a bit of a walk down memory lane.

Wired equivalent privacy

During September, 1999, the WEP security algorithm was created. **Wired Equivalent Privacy** (**WEP**), as the name suggests, was supposed to be as secure as wired Ethernet networks. At one point of time, it was the most used security algorithm. This was due to the fact that it was backwards compatible and was the first choice in the early router control options.

The early versions of WEP were particularly weak as the US Government had restrictions on the export of cryptographic technology that used greater than 64-bit encryption. This led the manufacturers to restrict themselves to the 64-bit encryption.

Once the US Government lifted the restrictions, 128-bit and 256-bit encryptions were introduced. However, most deployments of WEP happened with 128-bit decryption. While both 128 bit and 256 bit encryptions increased the key space and supposedly enhanced the security, the actual fact was that WEP was found to have numerous security holes and flaws. WEP networks were extremely vulnerable and easy to exploit with freely available software. In 2004, WEP was officially retired by the **Wi-Fi Alliance**.

Wi-Fi protected access

WEP was formally replaced with **Wi-Fi Protected Access** (**WPA**) in 2003 (a year before WEP was finally phased out) due to the increasing vulnerabilities and security flaws being discovered in the WEP standard.

While WEP used 64-bit and 128-bit keys, the keys used by WPA-PSK are 256-bit, which is a significant increase over the previous protocol.

Since WPA was born out of the need to implement stronger security, significant additional changes were implemented. To find out whether an **man-in-the-middle** (**MITM**) attack has compromised the integrity of the data being transmitted, message integrity checks and **Temporal Key Integrity Protocol** (**TKIP**) were added. WEP used a fixed key system; TKIP employed a per-packet key system thus, really increasing the security quite dramatically. Further security enhancements led to the **Advanced Encryption Standard** (**AES**) in addition to or superseding TKIP. TKIP was actually designed to be set up via firmware upgrades on the existing WEP devices, therefore, it had certain elements for compatibility purposes, which led to its exploitation.

While a number of attacks have been demonstrated against WPA, one of the most common ways that WPA has been breached is via the supplementary Wi-Fi protected system. The Wi-Fi protected system is essentially provided on Wi-Fi devices for the purpose of making connectivity to **wireless access points** (**WAPs**) easy.

WPA was officially superseded by WPA2 in 2006.

Wi-Fi Protected Access II

WPA was significantly changed to its new avatar, WPA2, by including the mandatory use of the more secure AES algorithm.

WPA2 still has some obscure vulnerabilities (however, a lot less than WPA), which requires an intruder to have insider access to the secured network in order to gain access to the security keys.

That said, the biggest vulnerability for WPA2 networks remains the same as that of WPA networks, namely, the **Wi-Fi Protected Setup** (**WPS**) implementation. Though it does take between 2-10 hours (depending upon your infrastructure) to break into a WPA/WPA2 network, the security risk is real and cannot be ignored. Ideally, WPS should be disabled on the device and if possible, the firmware flashed to eliminate WPS altogether.

The various iterations of the WEP, WPA, and WPA2 are shown in the following table. This table sums up their security rankings in a nutshell (as of now) for quick reference:

Sr. No.	Description	Security rank (1 is best)
1	WPA2 + AES	1
2	WPA + AES	2
3	WPA + TKIP/AES	3
4	WEP	4
5	Open network	5

The best options to implement, from a security perspective, are WPA2 + AES, along with disabling WPS. Everything else is on a sliding scale after that, with WEP being just a single step above a completely open network.

Securing your Wi-Fi network

Wi-Fi security isn't as straightforward as that of a normal network. Essentially, this is because every device that is a part of the network is also accessible from both within and outside the network.

Thus, any compromised device can open the gate to the complete network. That is definitely not a bridge you want an outsider to cross.

Wi-Fi security is not a small affair and requires serious thought and planning on the part of the implementation team.

Let's outline some of the following important security aspects to consider:

- **Turn on/Upgrade your Wi-Fi encryption**: As we had discussed in the earlier section, we must ensure that our network encryption is at the highest possible level for our network. WPA2 + AES with WPS turned off is the preferred option as of now.

- **Change your router password**: Keeping the default password same as the one that came from the manufacturer is a cardinal sin in the world of security. In fact, the Internet has lists of the default usernames and passwords of just about every router that is ever manufactured. Some of these can be found at the following:

  http://www.cirt.net/passwords

  http://www.routerpasswords.com

  http://www.portforward.com/default_username_password

- **Update router firmware and consider an upgrade to third party firmware if possible**: Ideally, the router should be running the latest firmware especially, if the firmware eliminates the WPS option. Alternatively, it is worth considering an upgrade to third-party firmware, such as **Tomato** or **DD-WRT**.

- **SSIDs – To Hide or Not to Hide?**: Routers are routinely shipped with the default SSIDs set by the manufacturer, such as **Netgear**. To a determined miscreant, it doesn't make any difference whether you hide an SSID or not, there are a number of tools out there that allow us to identify the hidden SSIDs. However, it does make sense to rename the SSID to something that does not give away the make/model as well any information related to the owner, such as the company name, address, and so on. All these pieces of information can be quite useful to a person planning to target you from both inside and outside. This only works on the principle of *security by obscurity*; wherein the security is dependent on not being found out. Tools such as **kismet** and **kisMAC** can detect hidden SSIDs.

- **MAC filtering**: This is an option that allows only specific computers (as defined by the MAC addresses) to access your Wi-Fi network. The MAC address is a unique ID that is assigned to every **network interface card (NIC)**. Unfortunately, any data sent in a packet carries a header, which lists out the MAC address of the NIC that is sending it. This makes it really easy for a hacker to spoof any allowed network card and get unfettered access to the Wi-Fi network.

Discussing common attacks on Wi-Fi networks

Prevention, detection, and investigation of illegal network activity is greatly strengthened by an intimate knowledge of the different modes of unauthorized access. The security perimeter of a Wi-Fi network is quite porous and breaches can come from multiple vectors.

To help enhance this knowledge, let's discuss the common attacks on Wi-Fi networks.

Incidental connection

When a user turns on his laptop and his device accidentally associates itself with an available Wi-Fi network (maybe due to the network being open), this is known as an incidental connection. The user may be unaware that this has occurred. This can be classified as an attack since the laptop may also be connected to another wired network and could perhaps provide inroads to this network from the *open* network. This *mis-association* could be accidental or deliberate with malicious intent, for example, the attacker's objective may be to bypass the company firewall and allowing a company employee to connect to this *open* network would help them achieve just that as the laptop would be a part of the trusted network. Therefore, beware of *free* or *open to air* Wi-Fi!

The following image represents an incidental connection:

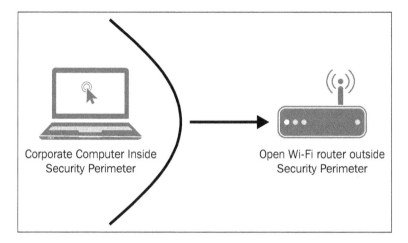

Malicious connection

Whenever an active connection with an unauthorized device is made to a corporate network with an employee's laptop acting as a *rogue access point* rather than the company's **access point** (**AP**). In such cases, the miscreant runs special tools, which makes their wireless network card look like a genuine access point. Once the miscreant has gained required access, stealing valuable information, grabbing passwords, or planting Trojans will be a piece of cake for them. These types of attacks occur when the miscreant successfully takes over a client. This could also happen in situations with an insiders involvement or help. The following image represents a malicious connection:

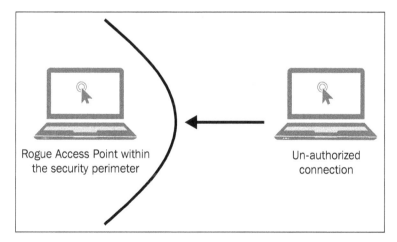

Ad hoc connection

Ad hoc connections can also pose a very serious security threat. These are defined as direct peer-to-peer connections between two devices without the presence of a wireless access point. In the wired world, one would consider this akin to a connection between two computers using a cross-over Ethernet cable.

An ad hoc connection establishes a bridge between the two connections thus, opening the secure corporate network to the outside world. This could be compromised in a number of ways, including access to and cracking passwords of corporate resources. This could happen by simply leaving a malicious code on the peer-connected computer, which could steal resources/information at appropriate times. This following image represents an ad-hoc connection:

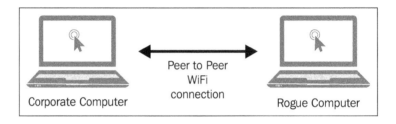

Non-traditional connections

Networks such as Bluetooth or **Bluetooth Low Energy** (**BLE**) qualify under this category. As these are not strictly Wi-Fi, they may not seem that dangerous; however, these are another vector to examine from a security breach perspective. Similar to the previous peer-to-peer connections, networks can be compromised by accessing a corporate computer over a Bluetooth connection. Other devices may also be available over BLE connections, which could help in compromising the security of the network.

Spoofed connections

As part of the overall security posture, network administrators tend to add MAC address filtering on Wi-Fi networks. However, MAC filtering is only effective in small networks such as **small office or home office** (**SOHO**) networks. Any network device that is on the air transmits its MAC address and therefore, can be easily compromised by any sniffer and a tool to spoof the MAC addresses.

Man-in-the-middle (MITM) connections

Any attack that uses a network device that is set up as an access point to entice unsuspecting users to log on with the objective of stealing their credentials is known as a **man-in-the-middle** (**MITM**) attack. Once this is done, the attacker sets up another connection using a separate network interface to a legitimate access point, allowing the traffic to flow through seemingly directly. One of the ways in which this can happen is using certain security faults in the challenge and handshake process to cause the previously connected computers to disconnect and then, reconnect to the hackers spoofed access point. This is known as a *de-authentication* attack. These kind of attacks are pretty common at public hotspots and similar locations.

The denial-of-service (DoS) attack

Any attack that continuously sends multiple requests (genuine or fraudulent) to a network device in such a manner as to prevent legitimate users from connecting to the network resource is called a DoS. From a Wi-Fi perspective, this means that users will be unable to log on to an access point as it has been flooded with bogus requests. The usual objective, other than the denial of actual service, is to have the network re-establish itself and broadcast all its credentials from scratch that allows a malicious hacker to gather all this information for an attack later in time.

These are just a small sampler of the many different attacks out there. Therefore, now it is the time to get ready to defend your turf...

Capturing and analyzing wireless traffic

Before we go off to dive into the deep waters of the Wi-Fi sea, it is time to invite our good seafaring friend, **Wireshark**, to the scene. Just as we had used Wireshark to capture traffic on our wired Ethernet networks in the previous chapters, we will now use it to capture the Wi-Fi network traffic.

Sniffing challenges in a Wi-Fi world

Sniffing Wi-Fi traffic can be quite challenging. Wireless networks work on multiple channels and use different frequencies, even in the same location. The challenge is to select a specific static channel. The next challenge is identifying the channel number that we have decided to capture.

Another important factor to consider is the distance between the point of capture and the transmitting point. The greater the range, the less reliable the collection. Interference and collisions can also affect the quality of capture. As discussed earlier, certain network frequencies are subject to interference by devices such as cordless phones and microwave ovens.

Configuring our network card

Before we begin sniffing, we need to manually set up our network interface in the *monitor mode*. Most drivers for Wi-Fi NIC's under Linux use the Linux wireless interface, which provides us the ability to configure the wireless card in the monitor mode. Unfortunately, Windows does not offer us that capability, therefore, we need to use specialized software such as **AirPcap** before we begin our capture. Of course, the best solution is to use a bootable distribution of Kali Linux. This has a plethora of open source tools that are very useful for all sorts of activities related to forensics and network security.

Sniffing packets with Wireshark

As in the case of wired (Ethernet) networks, we will use Wireshark to capture network traffic.

The following are the three different types of traffic that we may wish to capture:

- The traffic to and from our own computer and processes. To do this, we need to set our network interface (wireless card) in the *loopback* mode.

- The traffic between our sniffing computer and other computers on the network. Assuming that we are only interested in regular network data, rather than management and control packets; signal strengths; and data rates, then running a capture on our network interface without any special set up will be sufficient.

- The traffic that is *not* from or to our investigation machine. By this, we mean that our interest lies in capturing traffic between other machines on the network (not necessarily our own). We could also be interested in radio layer information, such as signal strengths and data rates, or 802.11 management, or control packets. To do this kind of capture, we would need to set our computer network interface in the *monitor* mode.

Before we take this exercise further, we need to understand the type of packets that exist. The 802.11 traffic has data packets (these are normal packets), management packets, and low-level control packets. Packets can be **unicast**, **multicast**, or **broadcast**:

- Unicast packets: Any network packet that is sent to a single destination is unicast. All IPv4 addresses are unicast by default, except the ones that are multicast or broadcast.

- Multicast packet: Any network packet sent to multiple destinations is multicast.

- Broadcast packet: Any packet sent to all destinations on a network segment is a broadcast packet.

To capture any traffic other than the unicast traffic, the wireless network interface will need to be set to the *monitor* mode. This can be done in most Linux and Mac implementations. Lets take a look at the following steps to do this:

1. The first step is to start Wireshark, as shown in the following image:

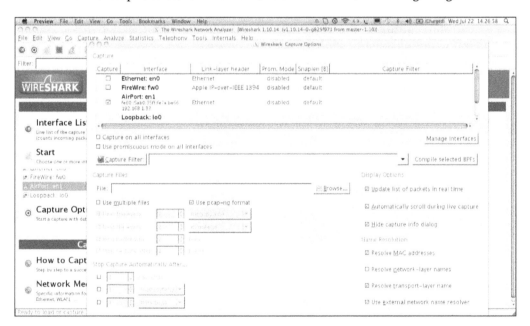

2. Next, we need to select the network interface that will be used for capturing the traffic, as follows:

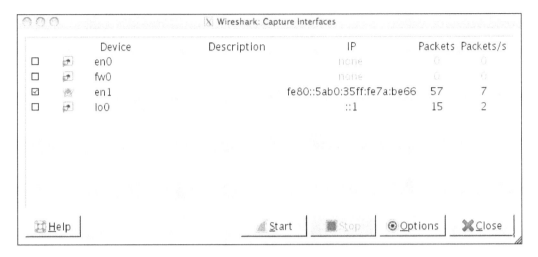

3. In our case, we will select the **en1** Wi-Fi interface. Once this is done, we can start capturing the traffic like we did with the Ethernet networks. The following screenshot shows a packet capture in progress:

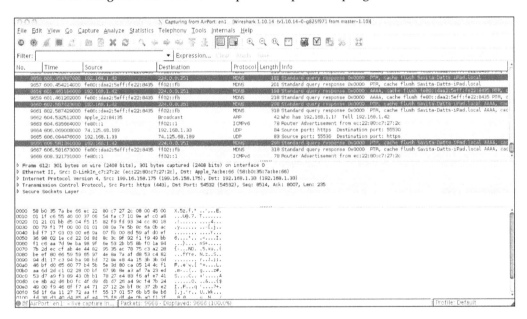

4. The moment we gather sufficient frames for the purpose of analysis, we can stop the capture and proceed with saving the capture to a .pcap file. To stop the capture, we will click on the red button shown in the following image:

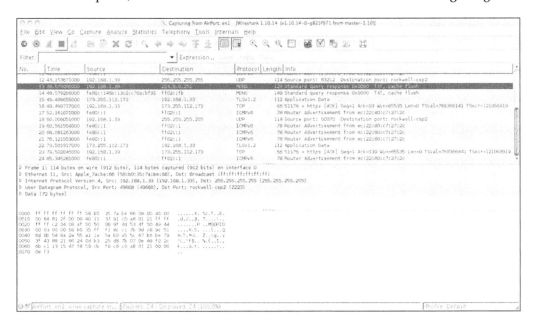

5. The next step for us is to save the captured frames or packets in a .pcap file. This is done as per the following screenshot:

This is quite important as the saved .pcap capture file can be analyzed in greater detail at a later time.

Analyzing wireless packet capture

Now that we have collected the evidence (or sniffed it, as in this case) it is time to mine through the data capture packets in order to make sense of the data that we have collected.

While it is very tempting to dive straight away into viewing the packet headers and contents, that will just end up confusing you as an investigator.

The best way to begin is to start by getting an overview of all the data that has been captured, baseline the environment, identify the focus areas, and narrow the focus using filters.

Let's start by loading our previously saved packet capture file:

1. Start Wireshark, as shown in the following image:

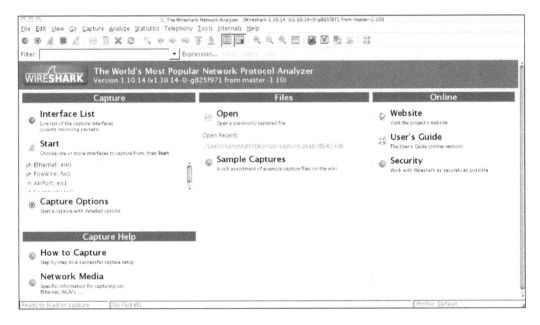

2. As we can see from the preceding screenshot, it shows us the recent capture we made. Let's click on this to load the data in Wireshark, as shown in the following image:

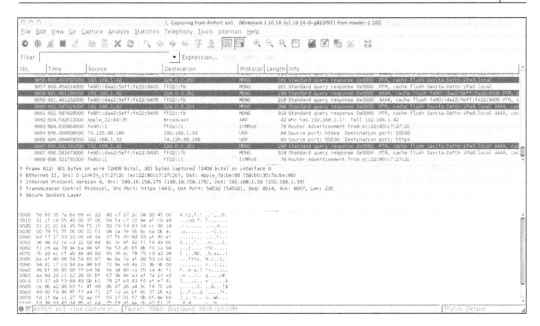

3. The preceding screen capture shows the captured packet file. Once we have the previously captured packet file loaded, we will navigate to **Statistics | Protocol Hierarchy**. You should get the following screenshot:

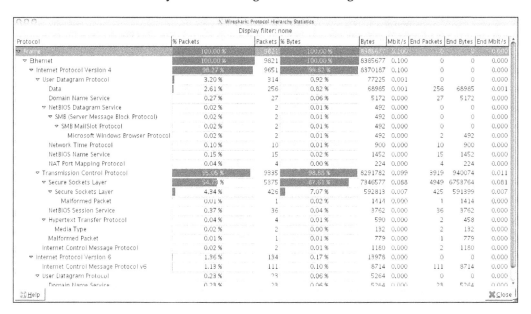

4. This helps us in understanding, at a glance, the kind of data present in our capture file. As we can see, in our case, most of the packets are TCP (95.05%), out of which 54.7% are SSL. There is a small percentage of malformed packets as well that we may wish to investigate.

   This information provides us a baseline from where we initiate our investigation.

5. To identify the different players in the captured session, we navigate to **Statistics | Conversations**. You should get something like the following screenshot:

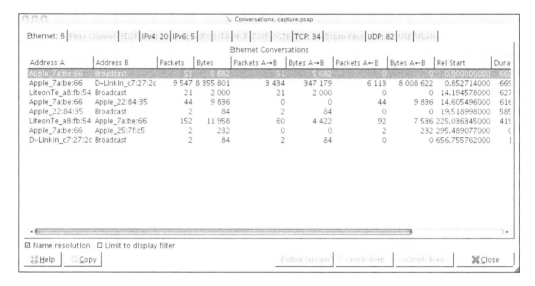

6. In the preceding screenshot of the conversations, the Ethernet tab shows the different pairs of Ethernet devices that are in conversation with each other in the segment of the network that we are monitoring. Again, this is useful information. Further, a closer look shows us which of the Ethernet device pairs on the network is the most active based on the number of packets received and sent.

We can carry out a similar analysis on the IP addresses involved in conversations with each other, as shown in the following screenshot:

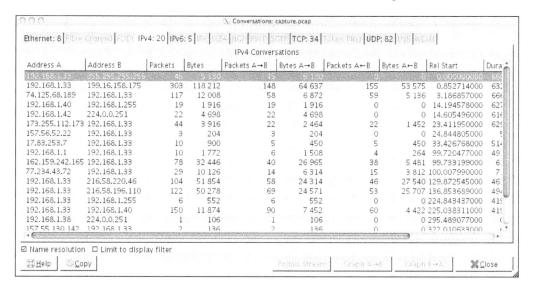

7. Another really useful feature that is built in Wireshark is the **GeoIP** feature. This allows Wireshark to resolve the IP addresses to actual cities and countries and even helps in plotting IP addresses on a map.

Geocoded IP address information in database form is available for use in both paid and unpaid versions at `https://www.maxmind.com/en/home`. When this is correctly installed and configured to work in these versions of Wireshark that are compiled with GeoIP code, it acts as a further enhancement of this already-powerful tool.

To determine whether the version downloaded by you is compatible with the GeoIP database, navigate to **Help** | **About Wireshark**.

In the window that pops up, there is a section that talks about the different modules that the downloaded version of Wireshark has been compiled with. If this mentions GeoIP, as shown in the following screenshot, then your version of Wireshark is set to go places:

8. Another very important aspect of analysis of packet data is that of filters. Using filters allows us to narrow down on investigation specifics.

As an example, if we wish to look at only the traffic that adheres to the HTTP protocol, we need to type `http` in our filters box. As we type in the box, the color of the box changes from red (unacceptable/meaningless input) to yellow (needs refinement) to green (acceptable). When we hit the apply button, the display will change to show us all the packets that comply with our requirement, as shown in the following screenshot:

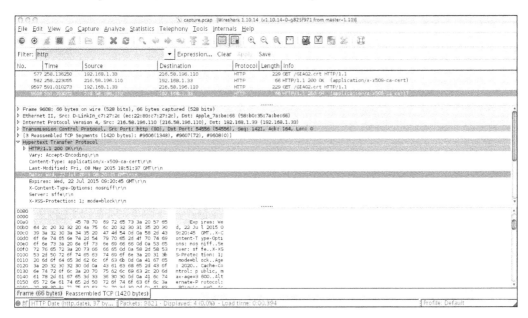

9. As we can see, the image only shows us pure TCP packets. If we examine the header of a selected packet in more detail in the middle pane, we can see the date information, from and to IP addresses, as well as the information related to the source and destination ports.

We can further trace the complete TCP stream by right-clicking on the packet to view this in more detail. The following screenshot shows us the options when we right click on a packet:

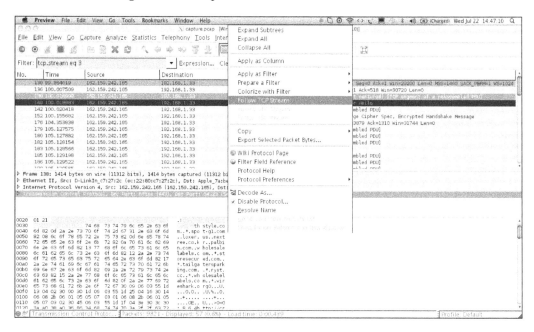

10. In this case, we will select **Follow TCP Stream**.

The output is as follows:

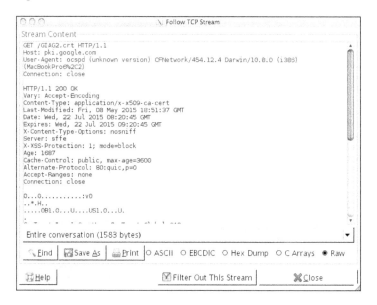

11. Every forensic investigator needs to have sharp observation skills. You would have all noticed that at the bottom left-hand corner of the Wireshark interface window, there is a red dot. This red dot indicates that there is expert information available for the investigator about the data that we sniffed earlier. When we click on this dot, the Expert Info window pops open.

This window, as we can see, carries a plethora of information, including errors such as malformed SSL and TCP packets, warnings, notes, and so on. All of these add to our knowledge about the various activities on our network:

Summary

As we have seen, Wi-Fi networks, while making life easier for end users, have increased our security risks correspondingly. The investigation of Wi-Fi data also involves a number of additional complexities such as ensuring the wireless network interface is in the *monitor* mode. However, once these issues are taken care of, capturing and analyzing Wi-Fi data can be quite straightforward and is just a matter of applying tools in an effective manner.

So far, we have made pretty good progress. In the next chapter, we will put together all that we have studied to track an intruder in our network. Therefore, put on your 007 hats and let's get started…

5

Tracking an Intruder
on the Network

"Beware the intentions of Uninvited Guests."

– Samir Datt

Intruders on a network are any network administrators' worst nightmare. Survey after survey conducted by the world's most trusted organizations point indisputably to the fact that, statistically, when it comes to network breaches, it is not a matter of *if* my network gets breached, but a matter of *when* my network gets breached. Some of the famous sites and networks that have been attacked in the past include the Pentagon, NATO, White House, and so on. As a network forensics investigator, it is critical to understand ways and means of intrusion detection and prevention.

Intrusion detection/prevention systems come in a multitude of flavors. There can be a host-based IDS/IPS or network-based IDS/IPS. Host-based systems monitor activity on the host computer, whereas network-based systems monitor activity based on network traffic captures.

This chapter focuses on detecting and preventing intrusions using a **Network Intrusion Detection System** (**NIDS**) and **Network Intrusion Prevention System** (**NIPS**). We will study their functionality and compare the differences between the two. You will also learn how to use the open source tool, SNORT, to acquire evidence in NIDS/NIPS mode from a practical perspective.

This chapter will cover the following topics:

- Understanding Network Intrusion Detection Systems
- Understanding Network Intrusion Prevention Systems
- Using modes of detection
- Differentiating between NIDS and NIPS
- Using SNORT for network intrusion detection and prevention

Understanding Network Intrusion Detection Systems

A **Network Intrusion Detection System** (**NIDS**) is a bit like the early warning alarm sirens that we see and hear in prison escape movies. These are triggered by a predefined event (such as an attempted break in/out) that is identified by a rule set enabled by the administrator/investigator. Just like a burglar alarm in a house, the NIDS is designed to detect an intruder and issue an alert to an authorized person.

Normally, a NIDS is able to detect intrusions in the network segment that it is monitoring. The key to its effective functioning is the correct placement of the NIDS device to enable it to monitor all network traffic entering and leaving the system. One way to do this is by placing it on the network and passing mirrored traffic through it. This is done to ensure that all the network traffic passes through the NIDS device.

The NIDS will monitor all inbound and outbound traffic and identify attempted intrusions by detecting anomalous patterns in the network traffic. This is done by identifying any known intrusion or attack signature, which is found in the intercepted traffic. A signature-based IDS is essentially a passive system that captures traffic, looks within the packets, compares content with known bad signatures, and raises corresponding alerts. This is depicted in the following image:

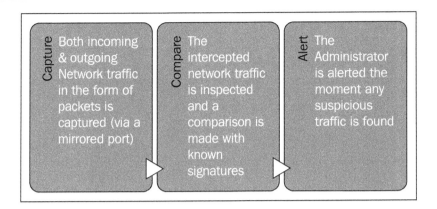

A typical IDS maintains a large database of attack signatures. These could represent signatures of attempted or actual intrusions, viruses, or worms. During its operation, the IDS will review all network traffic and compare it with the database of known signatures. Thus, any IDS is only as good as the quality of its signature database. A good-quality database will produce less false positives and is worth its weight in gold.

Let's take a quick look at the following table, which lists the type of alert states generated by NIDS:

Type	Event	Action	Description
True Positive	Attack	Alert	A genuine attack that triggers an alarm
False Positive	No attack	Alert	An event triggering an alarm even when no attack has taken place
False Negative	Attack	No alert	A genuine attack that triggers no alarm
True Negative	No attack	No alert	An event when no attack has taken place and no alarm is triggered

As we can see from the preceding table, both False Positive and False Negative are areas of great concern.

A false positive alarm takes up valuable resources to resolve whether the alarm is genuine or not. Consequently, a large number of false positive alarms could end up discrediting the IDS completely, allowing true positive alerts to be ignored in the general noise, and thus causing a lot of harm. A typical *Cry Wolf* situation!

False negatives are of much greater concern. When an attack slips in silently unnoticed, the time taken for discovery and, ultimately, resolution increases dramatically. This can cause huge losses to an organization.

Understanding Network Intrusion Prevention Systems

In the earlier section, we spent considerable time understanding NIDS. This has built a solid foundation, which we will find useful when moving on toward understanding NIPS.

Unlike a NIDS, which is a passive system, a NIPS is an active system that monitors network traffic and takes immediate preemptive action when a threat is detected. Intrusions are normally followed very quickly by vulnerability exploits. These are usually in the form of a malicious injection of data into an application or service with the objective of interrupting and gaining control of a machine or application. This could result in a denial of service (disabling applications or services), misusing existing privileges (rights and permissions) or escalating them for misuse, and gaining control of systems or resources.

In the information security world, most exploits come with an expiration date. This is because the moment an exploit has been identified, software vendors rush to patch it, signature-based IDS / IPS / security product vendors race to identify and remediate it, and every network administrator worth his salt moves to protect his/her network against it.

Hence, we see that unless a specific vulnerability is rapidly exploited, it will become inaccessible as an attack vector. Thus, in the world of digital intruders, time is of the essence. In such a situation, the NIPS plays a critical role in a network's defense line-up.

Usually, the NIPS is positioned directly behind the Internet-facing firewall. As this is inline, it actively analyzes all network traffic and takes automated action on traffic entering the network by dropping packets with malicious content.

Some of the actions that a NIPS takes are as follows:

- Notifying an administrator about the event causing the alarm; this action is similar to that performed by a NIDS
- Dropping the identified malicious packets
- Terminating the connections and blocking the source IP address
- Resetting the connection

Some of the key areas that a NIPS has to address are as follows:

- The network security (the critical function of countering threats and false positives)
- The network performance (the prevention of degradation by efficient and fast working)

Modes of detection

NIDS and NIPS use different methods to detect suspected intrusions. The two most common detection methods are pattern matching and anomaly detection.

Pattern matching

Intruder detection using pattern matching is also known as misuse detection or signature-based detection. Basically, this is used to detect known attacks by their patterns—this includes specific actions that happen as part of the attack or their "signatures".

This is similar to identifying criminals from the fingerprints they have left at the scene of a crime. However, to be able to accurately pinpoint the identity of the criminal who was present at the scene of the crime, we need to have his/her fingerprints available in our database. In the same fashion, we need to have the pattern or signature of possible attacks in our database before our IDS/IPS can detect such an event.

Hence, the effectiveness of an IDS that relies on pattern matching is completely dependent on the signature database. Therefore, in an IDS of this type, it is critical to keep the signature database completely up to date.

The greatest weakness of pattern matching is just this. Unless an attack's signature is present in the database, it will not be detected and will succeed very easily. Hence, the susceptibility of the network to *Zero* day attacks or even relatively new attacks is quite high. In addition, a number of common malware-based attacks exploit this weakness. These implement a minor modification in the pattern to get past the pattern matching, which looks for specific signatures. Hence, even if the attack is of the same type, the manipulated signature ensures that the NIDS and NIPS are unable to detect it.

Anomaly detection

Anomaly-based detection is all about the statistical comparison of normal usage patterns with deviations caused by attacks.

To begin with, a baseline profile is established to determine what is normal. Next, actions outside *normal* parameters are monitored. In this way, we can catch any new intruder on the network whose attack methodology does not have a known **attack signature** in our NIDS database.

This is similar to a night guard who guards a particular area. He knows from experience what is *normal* for the area. Anything he sees that does not conform to this normal baseline would be grounds for suspicion on his part.

A major issue with an anomaly detection-based IDS is the high incidence of *false positives*. This is because any behavior that seems unusual will be identified as an attack on the network.

A problem with anomaly-based IDS is the higher incidence of false positives because behavior that is unusual will be flagged as a possible attack, even if it's not. This can be mitigated in part by advanced heuristics and machine learning.

Differentiating between NIDS and NIPS

At first sight, both the solutions seem quite similar; however, there is a clear difference in that one is a passive monitoring and detection system that limits itself to raising an alarm at an anomaly or signature match, and the other is an active prevention system that takes proactive action when detecting a malicious packet by dropping it.

Usually, a NIPS is inline (between the firewall and rest of the network) and takes proactive action based on the set of rules provided to it. In the case of a NIDS, the device/computer is usually not inline but may get mirrored traffic from a network tap or mirrored port.

The network overhead in the case of a NIPS is more than that of a NIDS.

Another issue with a NIDS is that by the time an intruder hits the system and the administrator is informed, the intruder has already infiltrated the system to a good extent, thereby making a simple situation extremely dire.

While stability is paramount in both systems, the consequences of a NIDS crash are a blind area in the network security during the downtime. However, in the case of a NIPS crash, the whole network may go down with serious consequences.

IDS can be used in active mode, and this tends to blur the difference between IPS and an active IDS. An active IDS can be configured to drop packets based on certain criteria or even redirect traffic via a network device.

These days, there is a tremendous overlap between firewalls, NIPS, and NIDS. In fact, for some time, manufacturers have been working to combine all these into a single product. A number of these combined **Unified Threat Management (UTM)** devices are now available in the markets.

Using SNORT for network intrusion detection and prevention

SNORT is an open source intrusion detection/prevention system that is capable of real-time traffic analysis and packet logging. Extremely popular, SNORT is the tool of choice for the open source community. While there are a number of other NIDS and NIPS out there, we will stick to SNORT for the purposes of this section.

SNORT is available from the `https://www.snort.org/` website:

It makes a lot of sense to go through the documentation available on the website as this information is updated on a fairly regular basis.

At the time of writing, SNORT is available in flavors that run on some Linux distributions as well as Windows.

The download link will guide us to the correct flavor as per our requirements:

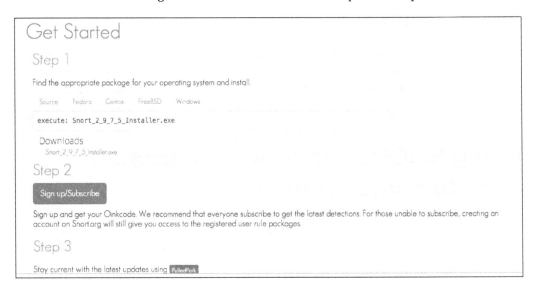

After the download, we need to install SNORT as per the following process:

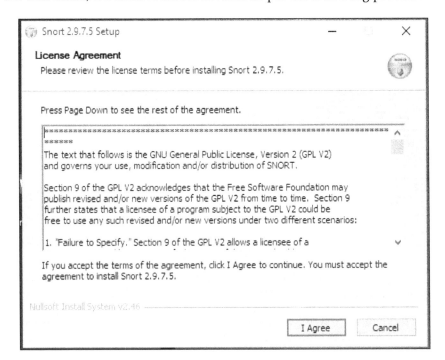

We start by agreeing to the GNU Public License (GPL) so that we can proceed with the installation of SNORT:

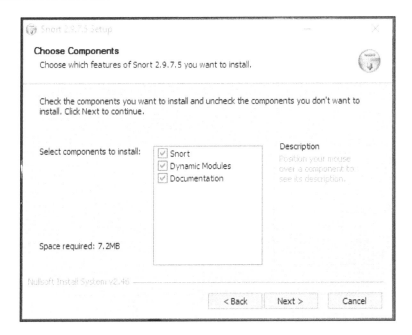

We then proceed to selecting the components that we need, and we are done:

The key step to follow after this is to edit the `snort.conf` file, where we can specify the proper paths for SNORT to look to for guidance:

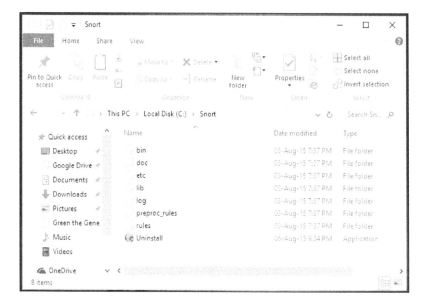

A text file editor such as vi editor or Notepad (for Windows) is used to edit the `snort.conf` file:

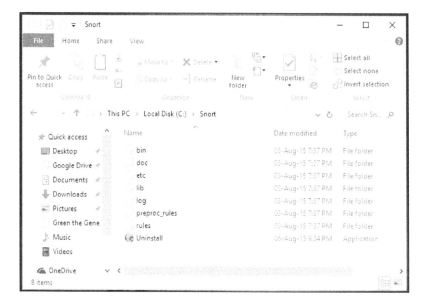

SNORT can be configured to run in three modes:

- The sniffer mode
- The packet logger mode
- The network intrusion detection/prevention mode

The sniffer mode

The sniffer mode just reads the packets and displays them in the console mode.

To get started, we use the following command:

```
./snort -v
```

This runs SNORT in verbose mode, shows the IP, grabs the TCP / IP / UDP / ICMP packet headers, and prints them out to the screen.

While -v shows details of the packet headers, we may feel the need to view the packet contents as well. To see these, we need to type the following command:

```
snort -vd
```

For details with extended data link layer headers, we can use the following command:

```
snort -vde
```

The following is the output for the preceding command:

The packet logger mode

The packet logger mode is similar to the sniffer mode, except that it logs packets to the disk. To enable it to do this, we need to set up our capture directory, where SNORT will store the captured packets.

By default, the SNORT installation creates a log directory in the `snort` folder. We can use this folder for the purposes of storing packet captures. The command for this is as follows:

```
./snort -vde -l ./log
```

In this case, we are asking SNORT to capture headers, packets, and data link layer information from all the packets and store them in a specified directory in the log format.

To enable logging relative to our home network, we can also specify to SNORT the home network using `-h` and the IP address range of the network, for example, `192.168.1.0/24`.

However, if we are going to need to view and analyze the packets later in another sniffer such as Wireshark, then we need to do the capturing or logging in the binary mode. To do this, we use the following command:

```
./snort -l ./log -b
```

SNORT also has the capability to read back these packets using the `-r` switch, which puts it in the playback mode.

The following is a sample log file created using the first option:

The network intrusion detection/prevention mode

The key to the effective use of SNORT for the purposes of intrusion detection or intrusion prevention is the SNORT configuration file usually known as the `snort.conf` file.

The command to get started quickly in basic NIDS mode is as follows:

```
snort -d -l ..\log -h 192.168.1.0/24 -c snort.conf
```

The following is the output of the preceding command:

```
C:\Snort\bin\snort -dev -l /log -h 192.168.0.0/24 -c ..\etc\snort.conf
Running in IDS mode

        --== Initializing Snort ==--
Initializing Output Plugins!
Initializing Preprocessors!
Initializing Plug-ins!
Parsing Rules file "..\etc\snort.conf"
PortVar 'HTTP_PORTS' defined :  [ 36 80:90 311 383 555 591 593 631 801 808 818 9
01 972 1158 1220 1414 1533 1741 1830 1942 2231 2301 2381 2578 2809 2980 3029 303
7 3057 3128 3443 3702 4000 4343 4848 5000 5117 5250 5600 5814 6080 6173 6988 700
0:7001 7005 7071 7144:7145 7510 7770 7777:7779 8000:8001 8008 8014:8015 8020 802
8 8040 8080:8082 8085 8088 8090 8118 8123 8180:8182 8222 8243 8280 8300 8333 834
4 8400 8443 8500 8509 8787 8800 8888 8899 8983 9000 9002 9060 9080 9090:9091 911
1 9290 9443 9447 9710 9788 9999:10000 11371 12601 13014 15489 19980 29991 33300
34412 34443:34444 40007 41080 44449 50000 50002 51423 53331 55252 55555 56712 ]
PortVar 'SHELLCODE_PORTS' defined :  [ 0:79 81:65535 ]
PortVar 'ORACLE_PORTS' defined :  [ 1024:65535 ]
PortVar 'SSH_PORTS' defined :  [ 22 ]
PortVar 'FTP_PORTS' defined :  [ 21 2100 3535 ]
PortVar 'SIP_PORTS' defined :  [ 5060:5061 5600 ]
PortVar 'FILE_DATA_PORTS' defined :  [ 36 80:90 110 143 311 383 555 591 593 631
801 808 818 901 972 1158 1220 1414 1533 1741 1830 1942 2231 2301 2381 2578 2809
2980 3029 3037 3057 3128 3443 3702 4000 4343 4848 5000 5117 5250 5600 5814 6080
6173 6988 7000:7001 7005 7071 7144:7145 7510 7770 7777:7779 8000:8001 8008 8014:
8015 8020 8028 8040 8080:8082 8085 8088 8090 8118 8123 8180:8182 8222 8243 8280
8300 8333 8344 8400 8443 8500 8509 8787 8800 8888 8899 8983 9000 9002 9060 9080
9090:9091 9111 9290 9443 9447 9710 9788 9999:10000 11371 12601 13014 15489 19980
 29991 33300 34412 34443:34444 40007 41080 44449 50000 50002 51423 53331 55252 5
5555 56712 ]
PortVar 'GTP_PORTS' defined :  [ 2123 2152 3386 ]
Detection:
   Search-Method = AC-Full-Q
    Split Any/Any group = enabled
    Search-Method-Optimizations = enabled
    Maximum pattern length = 20
Tagged Packet Limit: 256
Loading dynamic engine c:\Snort\lib\snort_dynamicengine\sf_engine.dll... done
Loading all dynamic preprocessor libs from c:\Snort\lib\snort_dynamicpreprocesso
```

SNORT can be run in three different modes:

- **Passive**: This is the default mode and SNORT acts as a NIDS in this mode. This is also known as TAP mode. Drop rules are not loaded.

- **Inline**: This is an active mode and SNORT acts as a NIPS in this role. This allows drop rules to trigger.

- **Inline-test**: This mode simulates the inline mode of SNORT, thus allowing the evaluation of inline behavior without affecting traffic and performance.

The real magic of SNORT is in the rules. Based on the rules, SNORT can be configured to give out alerts or take specific action.

Alerts can be in the form of the following:

- An output to the console or screen
- An output to a log file
- An output to a SQL database
- An output in the binary form for use with other sniffers
- An e-mail to an administrator

SNORT rules are divided into two logical sections — the rule header and rule options:

- The rule header consists of Action, Protocol, Source, and Destination IP addresses and netmasks and source and destination ports information
- The rule option section contains information and alert messages on the basis of which parts of the packet should be inspected in order to determine whether the rule action should be taken

The rule action options are as follows:

- **Alert**: This generates an alert based on the method selected and then logs the packet
- **Drop**: This blocks and logs the packet
- **Pass**: This just ignores the packet
- **Log**: This just logs the packet
- **Sdrop**: This just blocks the packet and doesn't log it
- **Reject**: This blocks and logs the packet, then sends a TCP reset for the TCP protocol or an ICMP port unreachable message if the protocol is UDP
- **Activate**: This sends an alert, and then turns on the dynamic mode
- **Dynamic**: This remains idle until activated by the `activate` rule, and then acts as a `log` rule

We can also define our own rule types and associate one or more output plugins for them.

SNORT currently analyzes TCP, UDP, ICMP, and IP protocols.

Making rules is better illustrated by an example. Let's assume that we wish to alert the administrator to all attempts by an intruder to telnet (Port 23) into our network.

For the sake of our discussion, let's say that our home network has the IP range from `192.168.1.0` to `255`. In such a case, we will write the following rule:

```
alert tcp any any -> 192.168.1.0/24 23
```

This means that any attempts from any network and any port to telnet into our home network of `192.168.1.0/24` would generate an intruder alert for the network administrator. This would show that an intruder is attempting to telnet into our network.

However, as we would like the alert to be a bit verbose and explain the attempt made by the intruder in simple language, we would use the rule options section and add some additional information, as follows:

```
alert tcp any any -> 192.168.1.0/24 23 (msg:"Intruder Alert - Telnet
used"; flags:A+;classtype:policy-violation;sid:100001;rev:1;)
```

In this case, the message `Intruder Alert - Telnet Used` would be flashed as part of the alert.

Let's take a look at another example. We have reason to believe that an insider in our organization is spending his time searching for obscene material. Our objective in this case is to alert the administrator to all attempts to use the network using port 80 with a search for the keyword, `porn`.

As we are aware, HTTP uses port `80`. Therefore, we will look for network activity from our network to any external network, which uses port `80` and contains the word `porn`.

To do this, let's write the following rule:

```
alert tcp $HOME_NET any -> any 80 (content:"porn"; sid:100002;rev:2;)
```

This rule will throw up all the searching and browsing activity with the word `porn` in it.

As we can see, SNORT is an extremely versatile tool, which gives us a lot of capability to identify both insider and outsider activity on the network. However, to actually use it to its fullest, it is important to considerably spend more time on practicing with SNORT. Entire books have been written on SNORT usage and rules. The Internet too has a number of excellent tutorials on using SNORT. As a potential network forensics expert and a Digital 007 in the making, I would recommend that you spend some additional time on this amazing tool. The SNORT manual in the PDF form (included in the distribution) is also an excellent resource to enhance one's capabilities and should be the first resource looked at by you.

Summary

In this chapter, you learned about network intrusion detection and prevention systems. We also explored how each has a different role to play and the different ways in which each performs its task. We have also been exposed to SNORT, which is a very versatile tool that can be used for both packet capture and network intrusion detection and prevention. You learned the importance of creating rules for NIDS/NIPS and explored how we can use these rules to identify intruders in our network.

In the next chapter, you will learn about a very important aspect of network forensics — connecting the dots using network logs. Just as a murderer leaves traces next to the victim's body, an intruder leaves traces of his/her activity in a network's log. Hence, the importance of network logs in any investigation is paramount. The next chapter will prepare us from this perspective.

6
Connecting the
Dots – Event Logs

"We need to connect the dots to make the invisible visible"

– Samir Datt

Just as we need to connect the dots to build a big picture, from a network forensics perspective, we need to correlate logs in order to get to the big picture of activity on a network. All devices that maintain logs of events are a great resource to track intruder activity. In our role as Network 007s, we will use these logs to try and track every step of the route taken by an intruder in our network.

Let's begin by trying to understand what logs are. A log, as the name suggests, is a record of information generated in response to a specific event or activity that occurs on a system or network. A log aims to capture the **who**, **what**, **when**, and **where** of an event. Logs can include the information about the date and time of the activity; device or application the log relates to; associated user or account; type of log—such as error, warning, information, and success or failure audits, and of course, cryptic or detailed information (depending upon how the logging is configured) about the actual event itself. Each specific event generates a log record. Multiple records form a log file, which is usually either in the text format or the records are stored in a database for easy management and analysis.

One of the typical problems that we face with log analysis is caused by the sheer magnitude of the generated logs. Depending on the number of devices and level of logging enabled, the volume can really add up. To tackle this issue, most logging systems are designed to store logs up to a specific period. Therefore, in the case of a firewall, we may have limited it to 10,000 logs of the most recent events or 100 MB of recent data by default, unless configured otherwise.

However, our perspective is different from that of a normal network administrator. Our aim is to detect, track, and identify intruders and illegal activity on our network. Therefore, an access to the older logs can be quite useful. A comparison of logs can produce interesting results. A simple example of this is a sudden threefold increase in the size of a log file. This itself can be an indicator of increased network activity, a possible indicator of a malware compromise.

Another major problem faced due to the volume of generated logs is that of manually analyzing the logs to look for anomalies. Wherever manual systems of log analysis are in place, over a period of time, we see that logs tend to be ignored. This can be remedied by the use of good log analysis tools such as Splunk and Logstash. We will examine Splunk's use for log analysis and visualization in this chapter.

In this chapter, we will cover the following topics:

- Understanding log formats
- Discovering the connection between logs and forensics
- Practicing sensible log management
- Analyzing network logs using Splunk

Understanding log formats

At the beginning of this chapter, we discussed how logs keep track of the four **Ws** related to an event. These were the when, where, who, and what of the event. Let's understand how each of these is done in a bit more detail in the following table:

	Attribute	Remarks
When	• Log date and time • Event date and time	The log date and time can be different from that of an event in some cases, such as in situations where the event data is remotely collected at intermittent times
Where	• Application ID • Application address • Service • Geolocation • Window/ webpage/ form	• Application name and version • System or server name, IP address, port number, and local device ID • Name and protocol • Latitude and longitude, where applicable • Entry-point URL, webpage entry-point URL, dialogue box, and so on
Who	• Code location	Path and name of the code module/script

	Attribute	Remarks
What	• Event type • Event severity • Event flag • Event description	• For example, log in, log out, access, delete, and so on • For example, critical, error, warning, information, and so on • Security relevant flags, for example, log in failures • Verbose description of an event, for example, **An account failed to log on**, with account name, security ID, domain, and a lot more information

One critical aspect in analyzing logs is that of *when*. Each log entry has a date and time input, which establishes the *when* of a specific event. Should this date or time be incorrect, all correlations will be hopelessly wrong and may end up completely messing up the analysis.

To illustrate this, let me share an incident that we came across in one of our investigations.

Use case

An airline received an *electronic* bomb threat for one of its long-haul flights scheduled for a particular date. This threat was communicated to the airline via its customer support/feedback page, which was hosted on its Internet-facing server. As was the norm, the data was collected by the web form and posted to an offshore support and feedback-handling center. The operator handling the complaint looked at the threat and notified her supervisor. Based on the supervisor's assessment, the threat was further escalated and both the airline and law enforcement were notified. To assist in the technical investigation of the case, our team was called in.

As a first step, we requested access to all the digital evidence as well as the logs of the web server, where the **Support Form** was posted. It was found that there was no record of the IP addresses used to send such e-mails. This itself was a major setback.

A quick look at the received communication established that the web Support Form sent the message in the form of a structured e-mail to the relevant support center. The headers of the e-mail were examined and the first thing we noticed was that the time taken by the e-mail to travel from the web server to the next SMTP server in a chain was slightly over 27 minutes. This seemed quite odd, therefore, we attempted to replicate the process by sending a test e-mail from the web form and found that, in this case, the time taken to traverse the same hop was just under one minute.

Confronted by this anomaly, we repeated the test numerous times and came up with the same result every time: under one minute. The 27 minutes taken by the original mail were unexplained. We approached the administrator with this issue and were informed that at the time when we had requested for the evidence, they had observed that the computer time was incorrect and not synchronized with the current time. Therefore, they had "fixed" this by shifting the time by "approximately" 30 minutes. This really threw a spanner in the works. We could no longer rely on the accuracy of the data in the header with respect to the time. To understand the impact of this "discrepancy", we need to realize that on a highly trafficked airline site, there can be a thousand visitors/hour. Therefore, an offset of about 30 minutes results in increasing the investigation window by about 500 visitors.

Time was short! The threatened event date was close. A herculean round-the-clock effort was put underway. All the web logs were acquired and an in-depth analysis of the logs was done. Approximate time offsets were incorporated with e-mail time and correlated with website hit logs and analyzed. Sixty-one suspect IP addresses were identified. The assistance of local **Internet service providers (ISPs)** was requested on an emergency basis. Each of the IP addresses was painstakingly identified and attributed. Two of these belonged to cyber cafes, which worked on a pay-as-you-use model. Cyber cafe owners assisted the local police in identifying the computers that were used at the time. Forensic images were made for later analysis. CCTV video was examined and some suspects were identified. Pictures were made and circulated to the airport security. At the same time, our forensic specialists examined the hard drive images and identified one of them as having being used to access the airline webpage and send the message. Any additional hard drive activity around the time of the webpage access was examined in detail. We found that the suspect had also accessed their personal e-mail account. Bingo—we had him! With a little assistance from the **Mail Service Provider (MSP)**, local law enforcement identified the suspect and picked him up for questioning. It turned out that the suspect who had sent the mail was a student. A friend of his was traveling in that flight and he had threatened him that he would not let his friend leave the country.

As you can see, this time the critical investigation could have had a considerably shorter investigation time had the server's time been synchronized properly. Indeed, it is recommended that a **Network Time Protocol (NTP)** server be deployed to maintain time across a network so that occurrences of this nature do not mar a network forensic investigation.

To understand the structure of a log file better, let's look at the standard by the **World Wide Web Consortium (W3C)**. (`https://www.w3.org/`).

The following is the structure of the Common Logfile Format:

```
remotehost rfc931 authuser [date] "request" status bytes
```

Let's understand each of these one by one, as shown in the following:

Term	Explanation
remotehost	This is usually the DNS hostname or IP address, in case the DNSLookup is off.
rfc931	This is an **Internet Engineering Task Force (IETF)** protocol that provides a means to identify the user of a particular TCP connection. This is known as the Identification Protocol. This denotes the remote logname of the user.
authuser	This is the user ID of the person requesting the document. This is determined by the username used for authentication.
[date]	This indicates the date and time of the request.
"request"	This is the request line from the client. For example, the client may request a webpage called forensics.html
status	This is the HTTP status code in response to the client's request. For example, a status code of 404 — means Not Found.
bytes	This is the size of the document returned in bytes in response to the request.

Let's assume that an outsider wishes to access a webpage called forensics.html on our web server.

The log entries that would be generated would be similar to the following:

```
216.168.5.3 - - [28/Aug/2015:13:20:39 +0530] "GET /forensics.html
HTTP/1.1" 200 177
```

```
216.168.5.3 - - [28/Aug/2015:13:20:40 +0530] "GET /image1.jpg HTTP/1.1"
200 431
```

```
216.168.5.3 - - [28/Aug/2015:13:20:41 +0530] "GET /image2.jpg HTTP/1.1"
200 2332
```

To put it simply, this means that a web browser based at the IP address 216.168.5.3 put in a request for the forensics.html page on August 28, 2015, at 13:20:39 hours IST, GMT +5.30 hours. The server responded with a successful response (200) and sent the file across. The file size was 177 bytes.

On receipt of this file, the web browser found that the webpage `forensics.html` had two inline images, namely: `image1.jpg` and `image2.jpg`. Subsequently, the browser put in a request for each of these images, which were successfully responded to by the server. The sizes of the images transmitted were `431` and `2332` bytes respectively.

Discovering the connection between logs and forensics

In the preceding section, we got a good understanding of what logs are like and the kind of data contained in them. I am sure that like any good investigator, we have a gut feeling that these can be pretty important. Let's work towards discovering exactly why this is so.

As we saw in the previous section, a log entry reflects an event that occurred in an organization's network. A group of log entries make a log file. Many such log files are directly related to the security, while others may have some entries specific to security-related matters. Security-related logs could be generated by anti-virus tools, firewalls, **intrusion detection and prevention systems (IDPS)**, operating system, networking equipment and applications, and so on.

The key factors to understand is that logs are a human-independent record of system and user activity in a network. This makes them particularly unbiased and allows for court admissibility as evidence, provided that they are collected, handled, and preserved in an acceptable manner. Logs provide the telltale fingerprints in an incident. They can tell us what happened, the sequence of the events, which systems were affected/involved, what information was compromised/what was not, how did the users caused or responded to the incident, and the time frame all this occurred in.

Logs are broadly classified as security logs, system logs, and application logs.

Security logs

Just about any organization worth its salt has a number of security measures in place. Each of these produces logs. These can include the following:

- **Anti-virus/anti-malware software**: This records the information related to various viruses, malware, rootkits, date and time of detection, systems it has been first detected in, disinfection/deletion attempt, quarantine action, and so on.

- **Routers**: Routers are usually the first line of defense in many networks. These are configured to allow or block specific network traffic based on the policies implemented by the network administrators. A study of the logs of blocked traffic can be useful from the forensics perspective.

- **Firewalls**: Just like routers, firewalls allow or block network activity based on the implemented policy; however, the methods used to examine the network traffic are much more sophisticated. This can include tracking of the state of network traffic and content inspection. The main difference between routers and firewalls lies in the more complex policies and more detailed activity logs vis-à-vis routers.

- **Intrusion detection and prevention systems**: As you learned in the previous chapter, **intrusion detection systems** (**IDS**) and **intrusion prevention systems** (**IPS**) identify, record, detect, and prevent suspicious behavior and attacks. As IPS systems are proactive, they may drop packets that are malicious in nature. Verbose logging of such packets is extremely useful from an investigation perspective. Logs of integrity-checking exercises performed by an IDS can also contain valuable information, especially when compared with the previous checks performed some time ago. This can help the forensic expert establish the time frame of the incident.

- **Remote access software**: Microsoft **Remote Desk Protocol** (**RDP**), LogMeIn, TeamViewer, and RADmin are a number of remote access software tools available that grant secured remote access through **virtual private networking** (**VPN**). A number of these VPN systems support granular access control (such as **Secure Sockets Layer** or **SSL**) and usually maintain detailed logs relating to the resource use that include date and time of access by the user, data transferred, as well as the details of all successful and failed login attempts. Information from these logs can help in identifying data theft and other remote activity, including unauthorized access.

- **Web proxies**: A number of organizations use web proxies to enable, monitor, filter, and restrict website access for their users. Web proxies also cache copies of the commonly requested webpages in order to make frequent accesses more efficient. Web proxies are designed to keep a record of all **Uniform Resource Locators** (**URLs**) accessed through them. As we can see, web proxies can help us in identifying where one of our users picked up an undesirable drive by download.

- **Vulnerability management software**: Thousands of vulnerabilities are discovered every year. This means that every organization has to constantly update and patch its environment. To do this on any scale requires specialized software for the job. This specialized vulnerability management software plays the dual role of patch management software and vulnerability assessment. Typically, vulnerability management system logs patch the installation history and vulnerability status of each host. This includes known/previously identified vulnerabilities in the software updates and may have information about the configurations of hosts. Vulnerability management software is usually run in the batch mode and generates a large number of log entries.

- **Authentication servers**: Whenever an entity (user or another computer) requires access to the network resources, its credentials need to be verified by an authentication server. Authentication servers include directory servers, single sign-on servers, an access point, or even a switch. These typically log every attempt at authentication: its origin, username, success or failure, and of course, the date and time.

System logs

Servers, systems, networking devices such as routers, and switches have their own operating systems. Each of these log a variety of security-related information. The most common are system events and audit records, as shown in the following:

- **System events**: From a forensic investigation perspective, system events such as starting a service, shutting down a system, or a failed event can be quite useful. All such events are usually logged with date and time, and could include status, error code, service name, and account associated with the event.

- **Audit records**: These store security information, including failed and successful authentication attempts, file creation, accesses, deletion, security policy changes, account creation and deletion, privilege escalation, and so on. The administrator can set the degree of detail captured in the logs.

Application logs

Applications are used to create, store, access, and manipulate data. The operating system provides the foundation for these applications while the role of the security systems is to protect this data. While some applications produce their own logs, some use the logging systems of the OS to log the data of relevance.

Some of the data that can be found in application-related logs is as follows:

- **Client/Server request and response**: These can be critical in reconstructing the sequence of events. If successful user authentications are logged, it is possible to determine the user who made the request. E-mail servers record the sender, recipient, e-mail subject, and attachment details; web servers record requested the URLs and response provided by the server; and financial applications record the records that were accessed by each user. All this information put together can be a treasure trove of evidence in an investigation.

- **Account-related information**: Logs can contain information related to successful and failed authentication attempts, account creation and deletion, account privilege escalation, and actual use of privileges. These logs help in identifying events such as brute-forcing password attempts as well as identifying when and by whom was the application used.

- **Usage-related information**: Information such as the number of transactions per hour (or minute) and the specific size of each transaction (such as e-mail size, file upload size, and so on) can be found in such logs. We can use this to identify a sudden increase in e-mail traffic, which might be indicative of a virus or malware or the download of large files (such as movies) in violation of the company policy.

- **Significant actions-related information**: This can include application start, shutdown, failures, as well as major application configuration changes.

Practicing sensible log management

The success of any kind of forensic investigation hinges on the preparation. As we have seen, logs are the mother lode of information and without them, network forensics would be seriously crippled. Criminals also realize this. Once a perpetrator has gained access to our network, one of the first things they try to do is cover the tracks. The first step in this process is getting rid of the logs that document their activity in first attempting and then succeeding in breaching the security of the network. To counter this risk, sensible log management processes have to be in place.

In every organization, there are a multitude of operating systems, a variety of security software, and a large number of applications; each of which generate logs. All this makes log management very complicated. Some of the problems associated with log management are as shown in the following:

- **Multiple log sources**: Logs can be generated on multiple hosts throughout the organization. Further, some applications can generate multiple logs, for example, authentication information can go into one log and application usage could be stored in another.

- **Inconsistent log file structure**: Different sources use different formats for their log files. Logs can be stored in **Comma Separated Values (CSV)**, **tab-separated values (TSV)**, databases, **Extensible Markup Language (XML)**, syslog, **Simple Network Markup Protocol (SNMP)**, and binary (as in the case of Windows) files.

- **Inconsistent data field representations**: Different logs represent different content differently. Some logs would identify a host using its IP address, while another would use the username. This could make it difficult to correlate the two though they represent the same entity. Another issue is how the data values are presented, for example, dates could be stored in the MMDDYYYY or MM-DD-YYYY format. Similarly, one system could log the use of the **File Transfer Protocol (FTP)**, while another could just identify it by its port number – 21.

- **Inconsistent timestamps**: While just about every log entry has a timestamp, the system generating the timestamp references its own internal system clock. Therefore, if the internal clock is inaccurate, the timestamp will also be inaccurate. This is a recipe for disaster. In the event of inconsistency between multiple security systems logs, an analysis of the sequence of events in a security breach can become seriously messed up.

- **Large volumes of data**: Any organization of a reasonable size can generate large volumes of logs in its network. Multiple sources and limited local storage compound the problem. Log file sizes are usually limited by the number of entries or size. However, this may not suit us from an investigation perspective. Therefore, it becomes imperative to have a way of collecting and storing logs for longer periods in separate locations.

The essential components of a forensic-friendly log management system include log management infrastructure and log management planning and policies.

Log management infrastructure

Network forensic investigations heavily rely on the logs to unravel a case. This is usually post mortem or after the event. If effective infrastructure is not in place and the required logs are unavailable, the investigation can be derailed or at the very least, seriously hampered.

A log management infrastructure typically has a layered three-tier structure as shown in the following image:

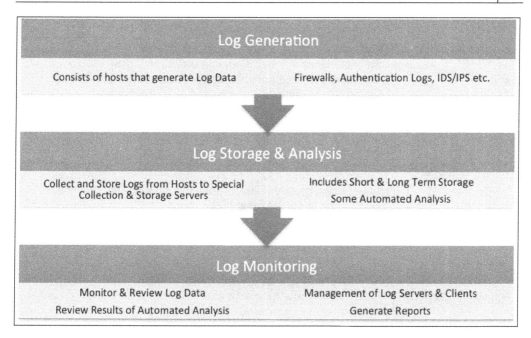

Log management infrastructure is required to perform a number of functions in a manner that does not change (or affect the integrity of) logs in any way.

Some of the typical log management infrastructure functions are as follows:

Function	Explanation
log parsing	This involves extraction of data from a log and subsequently passing it on to another logging process.
event filtering	This involves filtering out the events that do not have any information of interest. This is typically done during the analysis, reporting, or long term-storage stage so as to not alter the original log.
event aggregation	This involves consolidating multiple similar entries into a single entry, while incorporating the count of occurrences of the event.
log rotation	This is implemented to keep the log file sizes manageable and the preserve log entries. This involves closing a log file based on a certain criteria such as file size or data related to a particular time period, such as a day, week, month, and so on, and subsequently starting a new one.

Function	Explanation
log archival	This typically involves storing logs for an extended period of time. This could be on a **network-attached storage** (**NAS**), specialized archival server, or removable media. Log archival could be a part of either a log retention or log preservation kind of exercise. Log retention is part of the **standard operating procedures** (**SOPs**) of an organization; whereas log preservation could be part of the compliance to regulatory requirements, an ongoing investigation with the objective of preserving data of interest.
log compression	This involves storing log files in a compressed form to reduce the storage space required. This is done in a manner that prevents modification to the meaning of the content.
log reduction	This involves the removal of unneeded entries in a log file to make it smaller.
log conversion	Subsequent to log parsing, a log file undergoes a change in format before storage. This is known as log conversion.
log normalization	This involves converting each data field into a standardized format for consistent categorization. For example, the normalization of the multitude of date and time formats to a single standardized format. This process is essential in order to be able to carry out correlations and other analysis in any form. This can be quite a challenging task.
log file integrity checking	This involves generating a hash value (using industry-standard algorithms such as MD5 and SHA) to establish and maintain the integrity of log files throughout the log management process.
event correlation	This involves finding relationships between multiple log entries. For example, identifying all the traffic relating to a specific IP address or proliferation of **Internet Control Message Protocol** (**ICMP**) traffic (pings) from a series of machines in the network to track the spread of malware.
log viewing	This involves the use of specialized tools to display logs in human-readable format.
log reporting	This is the displayed outcome of the analysis. Log reports can involve summarized consolidated dashboard outputs as well as the typical reports. Today, systems offer a drill-down capability to increase the granularity of reporting.
log clearing	Logs cannot be stored indefinitely. Based on SOPs, retention policies, and regulatory requirements, logs must be removed from time to time.

Log management planning and policies

For any forensic investigation exercise to be meaningful, the organization needs to plan ahead and define its requirements and goals relating to the log management.

These can be influenced by the regulatory environment, such as **Health Insurance Portability and Accountability Act (HIPAA)**, **Payment Card Industry Data Security Standard (PCI DSS)**, and so on. From the perspective of business continuity, a balance has to be maintained between the time and resources required and the reduction of the organization's risk profile. Aspects of log management that need to be considered when defining policies and procedures are as follows:

Log management aspect	Issues to be addressed
Roles and responsibilities	Roles and Responsibilities of the following need to be clearly defined: • System administrators • Network administrators • Security administrators • Incident response teams • Application developers • Auditors • Information security officers • **Chief information officers (CIO)**

Log management aspect	Issues to be addressed
Establish logging policies	Mandatory requirements and recommendations need to be defined for the following:
	• Log generation
	Which hosts & type of hosts will log?
	Which host components (OS / service / applications) will log?
	Which events to log (security events, logon attempt, and so on)?
	What information to be logged for each event (user name and source IP for logons)?
	What will be the logging frequency? (every time, every 100 times, and so on)
	• Log transmission
	Which hosts will transfer to log management servers?
	What data/entries should be transferred to the infrastructure?
	When and how often should this be done?
	What methods/protocols should be used for the transmission? (Bandwidth requirements for the transmission will need to be looked at.)
	How will the **confidentiality, integrity, and availability (CIA)** be maintained during this process?
	• Log storage and disposal
	How often will logs be rotated?
	How long do the logs have to be stored?
	How will the legal preservation requests be handled?
	How much storage space will be required? (Daily load, peak load, and so on need to be studied and catered for.)
	What processes will be followed for secure deletion/disposal?
	How will the confidentiality, integrity, and availability be maintained during the storage and disposal processes?
	• Log analysis
	How often will each type of log be analyzed?
	What are the steps to be followed once a suspicious activity is identified?
	Who will be permitted to access the log data and who will follow these steps?
	How will the accidental exposure of confidential data in logs (such as e-mail content/passwords) be handled?
	How will the confidentiality, integrity, and availability of log analysis and reports be protected?

Now that we understand the fundamentals behind the logs and their management, let's see how to analyze the network logs.

Analyzing network logs using Splunk

Now that we have the logs, it is high time we understood how to collect and analyze them from a network forensic's perspective.

The tool of choice is **Splunk**. This is a very versatile tool (it also has a free version) that offers users the ability to collect log files from multiple sources, index and normalize the data within, then carry out an in-depth analysis to look for anomalies, prepare reports, and visualize the results. Lets take a look at it:

Splunk offers the facility to import and index data in a multitude of formats. This includes structured data, web services, network devices, Microsoft servers, application services, the cloud, and a host of others. The following are the steps to download and start using Splunk:

1. To get started, we need to download Splunk from `http://www.splunk.com/`, as shown in the following screenshot:

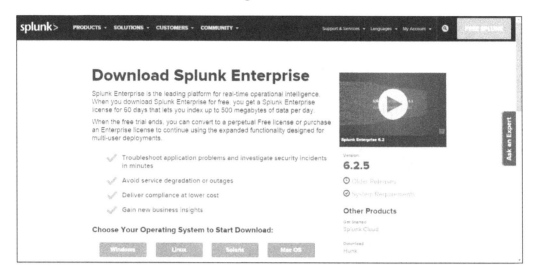

2. All we need to get started is to download the relevant binary based on the operating system that we intend to use for the analysis. As we can see in the preceding screenshot, Splunk supports Windows, Linux, Solaris, and Mac OS.

3. In our case, we will download the Windows binary so that we can collect the logs directly from the system itself and see whether we can get our hands on some interesting data.

4. Once the download is complete, Splunk requires the user to create a username and password. The password so created permits admin access to Spunk via the browser-based logon screen.

The next stage is to add data to Splunk, as shown in the following screenshot:

To do this, complete the following steps:

1. We click the first option, **Add Data**.

2. When we do this, we are provided three options as shown in the following screenshot:

The first is the upload option; this is to be selected when we want to analyze the log files that we have brought from the computer under investigation or have locally on our drive or removable media. In this case, the analysis is of the data of events that have occurred in the past and the log files are not changing dynamically. We can use this for the syslog files that are downloaded as a part of the tutorial on the Splunk site.

The second is the monitor option; in this case, we can monitor the ports as well as the files that are changing dynamically on the system. This is quite useful when we want to monitor the log activity in real time.

The third is the forwarding option. This allows multiple instances of Splunk to run on different machines. At one end, Splunk acts as a collector and at the other, it acts as a receiver. This helps in the collection and consolidation of logs over the network.

3. In this case, let's start by analyzing our own system's logs dynamically. The first step is to select the source of data. In our case, we will select **Local Event Logs**, as shown in the following image:

4. Once we do that, Splunk looks for all sorts of logs on the local system. Once these are identified (it takes only a few seconds), we are presented with a window showing us the logs that we wish to ingest into Splunk and then index for later analysis, as shown in the following screenshot:

5. We can select the logs one by one or add all at the same time. Once this is done, we move onto the **Input Settings** stage, as shown in the following image:

6. This stage is optional. Here, additional input parameters for the data are defined. In this case, we just accept the defaults and proceed to the **Review** stage, as shown in the following screenshot:

7. We review our selection and confirm that everything is as it should be. Once this is complete, our data import to Splunk is done. In the background, Splunk moves to the indexing mode, where it builds full in-depth indexes from the logs for high-speed retrieval, as shown in the following screenshot:

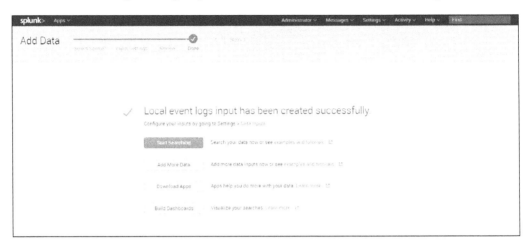

This is the stage where our long wait is over and we can indulge our 007 instinct. We can now begin to search for all sorts of *suspicious* activity. The Splunk **Search** page is shown in the following screenshot:

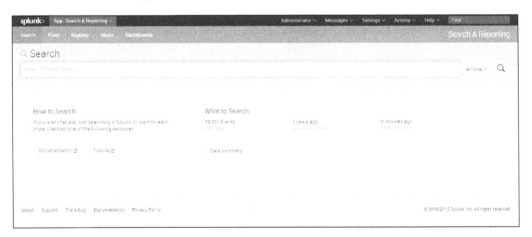

Just under it, Splunk lists the number of events indexed as well as the earlier and later event.

A quick click on **Data Summary** shows us the following result:

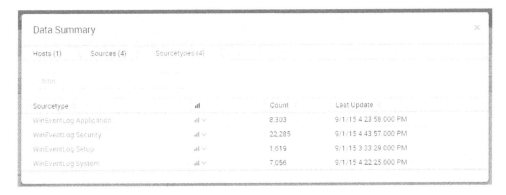

There are three tabs. The first **Hosts** tab shows that the data indexed by Splunk relates to a single host. The next two tabs show us that the data relates to four different sources and source types. Let's select the single host and see if there are any security events that merit our attention.

The good part about Splunk is that it has a Google-type search interface. We simply type in the text that we want it to look for and it shows us the results. In this case, let's look for the log entries that have the word logon as well a word beginning with pass. The wild card * denotes that the output that should include everything that starts with pass including passes and password (which is what we are looking for). It is shown in the following screenshot:

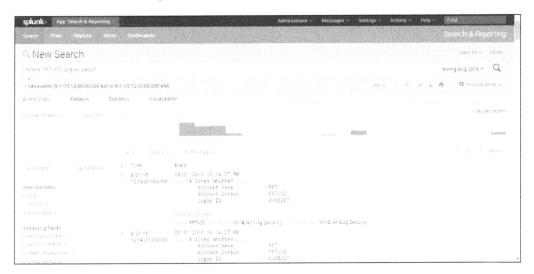

A quick look at the interface shows us that there are **149 events** that meet our criterion during the month of August, 2015. This is something we would definitely like to look at in more detail.

Let's expand these entries by clicking on the **>** sign on the left-hand side of the entry, as shown in the following:

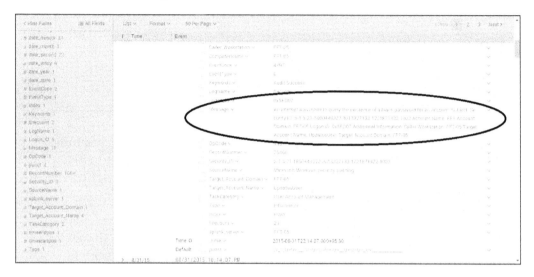

Suddenly, things have become a lot clear. If we look closely, we see that on August 31, 2015, at about 22:14 hours, an attempt was made to log on to the **FFT-05** host with a blank password. This is an example of the kind of interesting things that we are looking for.

While this reflects a single event, wouldn't it be great if we could see all the similar events visually. Luckily for us, this is what Splunk does really well. This aspect is called visualization and allows Splunk to aggregate the data and show it to us in an easy-to-understand graphical format. The following image illustrates this idea:

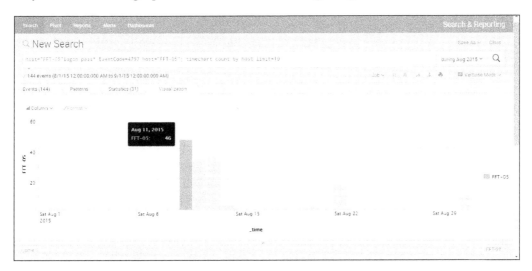

As we can see from the preceding image, our first attack began on August 11 and the latest was discovered on August 31.

This kind of information is quite valuable as it gives us an immediate insight into the kind of attack being directed at our information resources and gives us an excellent starting point to begin our investigation.

With a little bit of practice and the use of the excellent online tutorials available with Splunk, it is quite easy to gain the necessary expertise to begin your journey into log analysis and push your understanding of network forensics to another notch.

Summary

In this chapter, you learned about another valuable resource in our endeavor to understand network forensics. The importance of logging and different parameters in log management have been highlighted and discussed. We understood the questions we need to answer when we are setting up a logging system that will assist us at the time of a network forensic investigation. We have seen the importance of clock accuracy, correlation, collection, storage, and a host of other factors in logging. We have seen how getting multiple and disparate logs into a single log management system can help us connect the dots and give us an insight into the activities of the intruders zeroing in on our network.

In the next chapter, we will move on to another very important area from an investigation perspective. We will look at proxies, firewalls, and routers with a network forensic investigator's eye. We will see the different types of the preceding devices that form a part of our security perimeter. We will understand their functioning and study how to get data that is useful from this from a network forensic investigation's perspective.

7
Proxies, Firewalls, and Routers

"Every link in the chain has its own role to play."

– Samir Datt

Just as every link in a chain has its own role to play, every component in the network has a role to play and evidence to contribute to our investigation. In this chapter, we will exclusively focus on understanding web proxies, firewalls, and routers; reasons to investigate them; and how this would help in taking the investigation forward.

In this chapter, we will cover the following topics:

- Getting proxies to confess
- Making firewalls talk
- Tales routers tell

Getting proxies to confess

Proxies are a very important component of any network. A proxy acts as an intermediary between other computers of the network and the Internet. In simple terms, this means that all the traffic entering or leaving the network should pass through the proxy server. Looking back at our previous chapter, we recall that logs can be a forensic investigator's best friend. Proxy servers can generate such logs that we can use for our investigations.

Roles proxies play

Proxy servers are usually deployed with a number of end objectives in mind. They can be used for the following:

- **Sharing a network connection on a local area network**: Here, multiple users can share a single Internet connection.

- **Speeding up web access**: This shared Internet connection that is accessed via a proxy allows the proxy to cache regularly demanded pages such as Google. This enables the server to immediately deliver a page that is in the cache, speeding up the web access.

- **Reducing band width usage**: This local caching enables the server to reduce redundant or duplicate requests being sent out, reducing bandwidth usage and requirement.

- **Anonymity**: Proxy servers enable a user to hide their IP address behind that of the proxy. This also assists in preventing unexpected/direct access to user machines by machines that are external to the network.

- **Implementing Internet access control**: Proxies can also be used to authenticate users for Internet access or prevent users from accessing certain websites, to control usage during particular times, and as a web or content filter.

- **Bypassing security and restrictions**: A number of countries have Internet censorship in place that affects access to certain sites. A proxy server can help bypass these restrictions by making it seem that the connection originates from an altogether different IP address or location.

Types of proxies

Proxy servers come in all shapes and sizes. While some specialize in anonymizing Internet access, others focus on caching traffic to optimize the usage of Internet resources. To better our understanding of the proxy universe, let's take a quick look at the different types of proxies, as follows:

- **Anonymizing Proxy**: An anonymizing proxy is usually a web proxy that generally sits between the user and the Internet and works towards hiding or anonymizing the IP address and location of the Internet user. This is extremely useful for government users or corporates that do not wish to expose their information to malicious parties. This is quite useful for secure and anonymized communications as well:

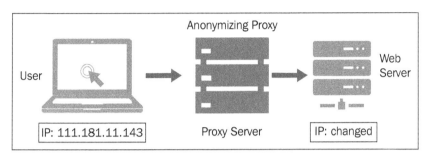

- **Highly Anonymizing Proxy**: As the name suggests, this proxy takes anonymizing to the next level. Not only does it hide the IP of the user, it also hides the fact that there is a proxy between the end user and the Internet. Unlike the normal proxy, the destination in this case does not know that it is being accessed via a proxy. To the destination, it seems as if it is being accessed by the client directly. The **REMOTE_ADDR** header contains the IP address of the proxy itself, which leads the destination to believe that the proxy is the actual client accessing it, as shown in the following image:

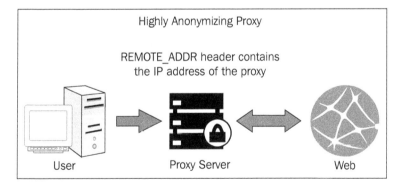

- **Transparent Proxy**: A transparent proxy is a proxy server and gateway rolled into one device. This is also known as an intercepting proxy. All the connections made by end users via the gateway are seamlessly redirected via the proxy. This does not require any configuration on the client side. As the name suggests, this forwards the request to the destination in a transparent manner, without hiding the client's IP address. Transparent proxies can be easily detected by examining the server-side HTTP headers, as shown in the following image:

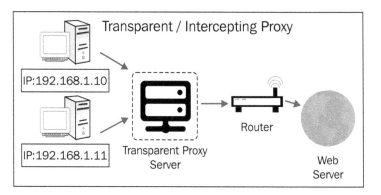

- **Distorting Proxy**: A proxy of this type correctly identifies itself as a proxy server; however, it intentionally misdirects by posting an incorrect IP address through the HTTP headers, as shown in the following image:

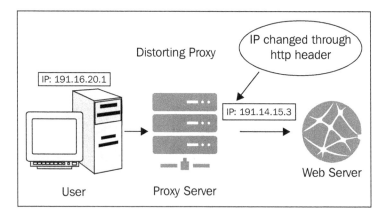

- **Reverse Proxy**: Reverse proxies are fairly common proxy servers that are positioned between the Internet and a firewall that is connected to the private networks. Requests originating from the Internet are received by the reverse proxy and directed to the network firewall. This prevents the Internet clients from obtaining unmonitored and direct access to restricted information stored on the network servers. When caching is enabled in a reverse proxy, the network traffic can be considerably reduced by providing the previously cached information to the network users without directing every request to the Internet, as shown in the following image:

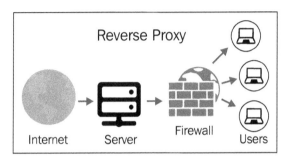

Understanding proxies

The evidence from proxies is usually in the cache and logs. If you recall, in the previous chapter, we spent a considerable amount of time understanding the logs, logging, and log management concepts. In this section, we will take a look at the evidence that we can dig out of them.

Before we begin, let's get a little familiar with some common proxy names that are available out there.

A few of the popular proxies include Squid, NetCache, ISA, BlueCoat, and so on. Proxies are available in both open source and paid varieties.

Comprehensive and voluminous books have been written about web proxies; however, as our plan is to focus on understanding their role and how to use them with our 007 hat on, we will select one and work at deepening our understanding of how it works and the kind of evidence we can get out of it.

For the purpose of this lesson, we will work with Squid. Squid is a very popular and versatile open source proxy that enjoys widespread usage worldwide. Squid is made available under the terms of the GNU General Public License. It is extremely flexible and customizable and works in both forward and reverse proxy scenarios.

Squid works by caching web objects of many different kinds. This can include frequently accessed webpages, media files, and so on, including those accessed through HTTP as well as FTP. This reduces the response time and bandwidth congestion.

A Squid proxy server is a separate server and works by tracking the use of an object over the network. At the time of the first request, Squid will play the role of an intermediary and will pass on the client's request to the server and in reverse pass, on the server's response to the client, while also saving a local copy of the requested object. However, for every subsequent request of the same object, it will serve the object from its local cache. In large organizations, this is the reason that system updates and patching takes a lot less time and bandwidth even when updating hundreds of machines at the same time.

The following graphic gives a pictorial representation of the Squid web proxy server in action. As we can see, it sits between the users and the router and plays a number of roles:

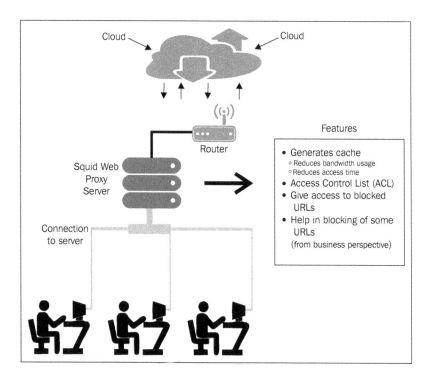

An amazing side effect of this caching behavior is the availability of (unexpired) items of evidential interest in the cache that Squid (or any proxy server, for that matter) has secreted away to improve the network performance. For us, items such as these can really help us in presenting the smoking gun.

In a case relating to sexual harassment at the workplace, an employee was identified to be downloading sexually-explicit material and sending it to a female employee using a colleague's e-mail ID. The idea behind this was to implicate that the colleague and harass the other employee. While the suspect's logs showed access to strangely (though seemingly innocent) named files hosted on the servers accessed through IP addresses (unresolved DNS), the cache had the actual corresponding content that proved that the suspect was the real culprit behind both the crimes.

In its role as a regular forward proxy, Squid provides the following functionalities:

- Caching
- Authentication and authorization
- Content filtering or Internet policy enforcement
- Network resource usage management

In the role of a reverse proxy, Squid can perform following functions:

- Sit in front of a server farm caching and serving static content
- Optimize the web server's usage while serving data to the clients
- Enhance security by web-filtering the content
- Act as an IPv4 - IPv6 gateway

Installing Squid is quite straightforward. The installation process involves three steps and though there are just three steps, they may slightly vary with different flavors of Linux:

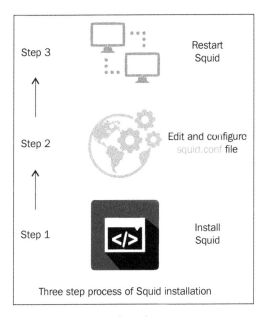

Three step process of Squid installation

The following screenshot shows its installation in Ubuntu:

```
sam@fgwkhorse: -$ sudo apt -get install squid
[sudo] password for sam
Reading package lists... Done
Building dependency tree
Reading state information... Done
Squid is already the newest version.
0 upgraded, 0 newly installed, 0 to remove and 64 not upgraded
```

We start by running the install command as superuser. At this point, our Ubuntu box asks for a password. Once this is provided, it goes ahead and checks whether Squid is already installed. If yes, then it checks to see whether it is the latest version, if not, it will upgrade it. In my case, as previously shown, it has done everything and found that I already have the latest version installed. This shows that we are good to go to the second stage.

The next stage is the modification of our `squid.conf` configuration file.

This file for Ubuntu is found under the following path:

`etc/squid3/squid.conf`

In other flavors of Linux, it can be found at the following:

`etc/squid/squid.conf`

In the previous chapter, you may recall that we had spent time modifying the `splunk.conf` file in order to be able to run Splunk effectively. We need to do the same here for Squid. To edit the `squid.conf` file, we open it in our favorite text editor and make the necessary changes, as follows:

`sam@fgwkhorse: -$ sudo vim /etc/squid3/squid.conf`

While there are a large number of changes that can be made to the `squid.conf` file to tweak Squid to run exactly as per our needs, a lot of these options are out of the scope of this chapter. Suffice to say, our idea is to get a feel of the topic and then go on to the investigative aspects.

By default, most of the settings in the configuration file do not need to be changed. Theoretically, Squid can be run with a completely blank configuration file. In most cases, if we start with the default `squid.conf` file (which we usually do), at least one part will have to be changed for sure. By default, the `squid.conf` blocks access to all browsers. We need to change this otherwise Squid will cut us off from the Internet.

The first thing to do in the configuration file is to set the HTTP port(s) on which Squid will listen for incoming requests. By default, this is set to 3128.

As we are aware, network services listen at particular ports for requests directed at them. Only system administrators have the right to use ports under 1024. These are used by programs that provide services such as POP, SMTP, HTTP, DNS, and so on. Port numbers that are greater than 1024 are considered as belonging to non-admin untrusted services as well as transient connection requests such as those related to outgoing data.

The **Hypertext Transfer Protocol (HTTP)** typically uses port 80 for listening for incoming web requests. A lot of ISPs use port 8080 as a sort of pseudo-standard for the HTTP traffic.

As you learned a bit earlier, Squid's default HTTP caching port is 3128. If we wish to add the 8080 port to our configuration, one of the ways to do it is to add it in the configuration file, as follows:

```
http_port 3128 8080
```

Another aspect to consider is the storage of cached data. As we have studied, one of the main roles of a web proxy is to cache the data to speed up the access and reduce the bandwidth usage. All this data that has to be cached must be stored, therefore, there exists a need for proper high-speed storage to be available for the proxy server. Depending on the throughput requirements, the hardware available to Squid (or any other proxy server for that matter) can make or mar an installation.

As part of the configuration process, we need to guide Squid by providing it information relating to the directories where it needs to store the cached data. This is done with the `cache_dir` operator. As storage requirements may vary and we may need to specify more than one directory for the cached data, Squid allows us multiple use of the `cache_dir` operator.

Let's look at the default values for the `cache_dir` operator in the standard `squid.conf` configuration file, as follows:

```
cache_dir ufs /usr/local/squid/var/cache/ 100 16 256
```

Let's take a quick look at what this means.

The line begins with the `cache_dir` operator. This allows Squid to know the path and name of the directory where the cache will be stored. This information is also useful for us as investigators. The way Squid structures this directory is to create another layer of sub-directories and then another to enable efficient storage and retrieval without sacrificing the speed. This information is reflected in the line that follows the following format:

```
cache_dir storageformat Directory-Name Mbytes L1 L2 [options]
```

Let's compare the two command lines.

We can see that UFS is the storage format, followed by the complete path and name of the storage directory, and then followed by `Mbytes` that is the amount of drive space in Megabytes to use under this directory. By default, this is `100` MB. It is usually recommended to change this to suit our specific requirements. It is not unheard of to add another zero to make the storage at least a Gigabyte.

The `L1` denotes the number of level one or first level sub-directories that Squid will create under the `Directory` specified earlier. By default, this is `16`.

The `L2` is the number of level two or second-level sub-directories that will be created under each of the previously mentioned first-level directories. In this case, the default is `256`.

The next thing to ensure is logging. We need to order Squid to log every request to the cache. This is done by ensuring the existence of the following line in the configuration file:

```
cache_access_log /var/log/squid/access.log
```

All requests to the proxy server will be logged as per the path and filename specified earlier. Again, these logs are very important to us from the perspective of network forensics.

Before we move on from the configuration setting in the `squid.conf` file, it is very important to touch upon network access control. This is handled by ACLs.

One of the issues that the Squid proxy server is required to handle is restricting access to any IPs that are not on the network. This is to prevent some happy traveler from a nearby network dropping in to take advantage of our open hospitality. The simplest way to do this is to only allow the IP addresses that are part of your network.

This is best illustrated with the example shown in the following:

```
acl localnet src 192.168.1.0/255.255.255.0
http_access allow localnet
```

By now, we should have a fairly clear idea of managing the Squid configuration file.

Let's move on to the third and the final step of starting the Squid server to enable and activate the configurations that we have done, as follows:

```
service squid start
```

That's all it takes! Now, we have the Squid proxy server up and running with the configuration that we set up for it.

We can verify its status by typing the following command:

```
service squid status
```

That's it! We can now move on to identifying and examining the evidence that proxy servers generate.

Excavating the evidence

As we saw in the earlier section, evidence exists in the cache directory and logs of the proxy server.

Some of the regular uses of a web proxy such as Squid include security, efficiency, compliance, user auditing, and monitoring. All this information is largely determined by the data present in the logs.

Logs allow us to see the following:

* User-specific web activities
* Application-specific web activities
* Malware activities that use HTTP

Let's look at the typical structure of logs generated by the proxy servers.

The `access.log` file basically has two possible formats depending on the configurations. The first is the default or native log file format and the second is the Common LogFile Format. In the last chapter, we had examined the Common Logfile Format to some level of detail, therefore, in this chapter, let's focus on Squid's native log file format. Each line represents an event or request to the server. The format of this is as follows:

```
time elapsed remotehost code/status bytes method URL rfc931 hierarchy_
code type
```

In this preceding line, every field has information that is of interest. Let's look at each of them one by one in the following:

Data Field	Type	Description
Time	float	This is the system time in the Unix format. Basically, it is a listing of every second elapsed since 1970. There are a number of tools and perl scripts available to convert this into something that is readable by humans.
Elapsed	integer	This is the time elapsed/duration in milliseconds to complete the transaction.
Remote host	string	This is the client address or IP address of the requesting browser.
Result Code	string	The Result Code generated by Squid is composed of a number of tags separated by the underscore character. This usually begins with any one of the following: TCP, UDP, or NONE to denote the mode by which the result was delivered. The next tag is an optional one and is usually separated from this tag by an underscore. An example of this would be the following:
		TCP_HIT: This means that the result was delivered using TCP (HTTP port 3128) and the HIT denotes that it was delivered from cache.
		TCP_MISS: This actually denotes that the result that was delivered was a network response.
		The Squid website (www.squid-cache.org) has an extensive documentation on the different Result Codes and tags comprising it.

Data Field	Type	Description
Status Code	**integer**	The Result Code is followed by a slash and then by the Status Code. These HTTP status codes are mostly taken from RFC 1945, 2518, 2616, and 4918. Some of these codes are informational in nature, such as 101 means Switching Protocols and 102 means Processing, while others are related to the transaction details and errors. For example, a status code of 200 would signify OK (a successful transaction), while a 401 code would signify an Unauthorized request.
Bytes	**integer**	Bytes obviously signify the size of the data delivered to the client in Bytes. Error reports, headers, and object data all count towards this total.
Method	**string**	This is the HTTP request method used to obtain the object. These include GET, HEAD, PUT, POST, and so on. Again, detailed documentation is available on the Squid site.
URL	**string**	This contains the complete URL requested by the client.
rfc931	**string**	This may contain the user's identity for the requestor. This information is usually obtained from either HTTP/TLS authentication, IDENT lookup, or external ACL helper. If no identity can be found, then this field will contain "-".
Hierarchy_code	**string**	**TIMEOUT**: This is a prefix that gets tagged if a timeout occurs while waiting for the ICP replies from the neighbors. **HIERARCHY CODE**: This code explains how the request was handled by the server. For instance, a response of DIRECT shows that the data was fetched direct from the main origin server, while a response of NONE means no hierarchy information, TCP failures, and so on. Comprehensive documentation is available on the squid-cache.org site. **IP ADDRESS/HOSTNAME**: This could belong to an Origin server, a parent of a peer caching server.
Type	**string**	This is the type of object requested, usually a recognizable MIME type; however, some objects have no type and are represented by a -.

Another point to note is that in the event the debugging option of **log_mime_headers** is enabled, all the HTTP request and reply headers are logged and there may be two additional columns in the access log due to this.

Now that we have a good idea of the structure of web proxy logs, we need to figure out how to use them in our investigation.

Some of the common investigations they are used for are as follows:

- Policy violations relating to the Internet access
- Monitoring user activity
- Tracking the spread of malware and spyware infections in our network
- Intruder attacks on clients and servers — both internal and external
- Detection of IP theft and leakage of information

Investigating proxy server logs can be a lot of fun. Just scanning about aimlessly through multiple logs can be quite diverting, but apart from enhancing the level of your understanding, it may not yield quick results.

Therefore, how do we go about looking for evidence on web proxies?

Let's begin with a particular scenario. We have an unknown user on our network, who is uploading our company's secret files (appropriately called `secrets.pdf`) outside of our network.

As we are aware that HTTP methods are used to determine whether files are being downloaded or uploaded. Whenever we send a request for a webpage or graphic, the HTTP method used is GET. Similarly, every time an upload occurs (for example, an e-mail is sent with an attachment), the HTTP method used is POST.

Just looking at all log entries, where the `HTTP method = POST`, will give us an insight into all the data leaving the network. Similarly, filtering `content type = application/pdf` in addition to the HTTP method will give us a list of the log entries where the PDF files have been uploaded out of our network.

Additional things to look for when investigating such activities include the following:

- Uploads to IP addresses that are not resolvable using DNS lookups
- Uploads to online storage sites such as Dropbox, iCloud, and Skydrive or hosts such as Hostgator
- Uploads happening via ports not equal to 80 (for example, upload to `10.10.1.7:31333`)
- Upload with the confidential filename in the log file entry itself

Similarly, a drive by download infection would be identified by a GET and when we look at the logs, we will find that executable files have been downloaded.

Another way is to identify the violation of company acceptable use policy by user downloads of video or music files is by looking at the downloaded file sizes and file types.

As we have seen that once we know what we are looking for, it becomes very easy to get proxies to confess.

Let's now move on to understanding and examining firewalls and the ways in which they can contribute to our forensic examinations.

Making firewalls talk

Simply the name, firewall, conjures up an image of a great wall of fire burning anything that is unauthorized and trying to pass through.

Just as the name suggests, in the digital world, a firewall prevents an unauthorized access to or from a network. A firewall is usually at the perimeter of a private network and the open Internet, it acts as a barrier and allows traffic through based on a set of pre-defined rules:

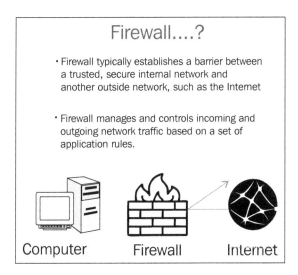

The preceding image clearly demonstrates the functioning of a firewall. As we can see, the network traffic can either pass through or be rejected by the firewall when found to be contrary to a pre-defined rule. The key factor of interest for us is the fact that every interaction with the firewall leaves a trace. This is reflected in the form of an entry in the firewall logs. Network forensic investigations require us to understand the firewalls and events that produce the entries in the log files. As the Digital 007s, it's our job to "make the firewalls talk".

One of the fundamental things that we need to understand is that a firewall is a system or group of systems that act as a bouncer whose job is to decide who enters or who does not enter our network. In simple words, a firewall controls the access to our network and this is usually based on a number of rules implemented by a network administrator. In addition to this, it plays a crucial role of keeping tabs on every one that accesses our network or even attempts to access it for whatever reason.

Some firewalls are designed to permit just a single kind of traffic through them, such as e-mails. While others may be configured to protect the network from unauthorized logins from the outside world. Firewalls can provide a single choke point to the network. This choke point can be used to implement effective security and audit rules in order to protect and monitor the network, as shown in the following:

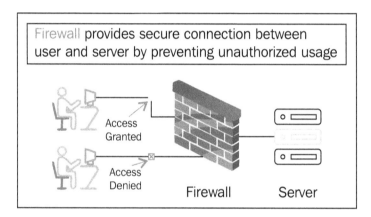

Let's enhance our understanding about firewalls by examining the different types of firewalls.

Different types of firewalls

Firewalls have a long and checkered history. They began their career as **Access Control Lists (ACLs)** embedded in routers that are still in use today to the new and highly touted **Next-Generation Firewalls (NGFWs)**.

Let's take a look at the different types of firewalls.

The **National Institute of Standards and Technology** (**NIST**) 800 - 10 broadly classifies firewalls into the following three distinct types:

- Packet Filter firewalls
- Stateful Inspection firewalls
- Application/Proxy firewalls

In today's networked environment, there is a fairly high degree of overlap with a number of commercial products having features of all the three categories as well.

Packet filter firewalls

These firewalls determine the access to internal or external resources based on the Access Control Lists. Filtering may be on the basis of source or destination IP addresses, ports, protocols, time range, and so on. All this information is available in the packet header. The packet filter examines the header and based on a specified set of rules (ACLs), this decides whether to allow it to go through (ACCEPT) or stop it from passing (DROP), as shown in the following image:

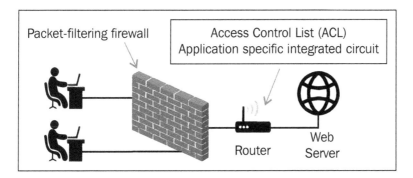

One key point to remember is that such firewalls have **NO** insight into the packet content and makes its decision to allow or disallow specific packets based on the packet-header conformance to the ACL's setup at the time. These firewalls operate at the network level of the OSI model.

However, their weakness lies in their very nature. Let's take a situation where the ACL in use allows an open port 80. This is fairly common as this is used for HTTP (www) requests. Any malicious user can setup their packets to be crafted so that they are directed to port 80 and are routinely passed through.

While these firewalls have been around for a long time, they should not be discounted. They are fairly widespread, provide a very fast response, and are a part of an organization's defense in depth security stance.

Stateful inspection firewalls

Stateful inspection firewalls were the next major evolutionary step. One major weakness in the packet filter type of firewalls was the their ability to be fooled by the information in the header. While they would look at and analyze a packet with SYN in the header, they would allow a packet with an ACK right through, assuming that it was in response to the SYN of a previous packet. This allowed malicious individuals to craft specialized packets with ACK configured so that the firewall just let the packet through. This was due to the fact that the packet filter firewall did not maintain a record of the state of communications between devices. Therefore, stateful packet inspection firewalls were born:

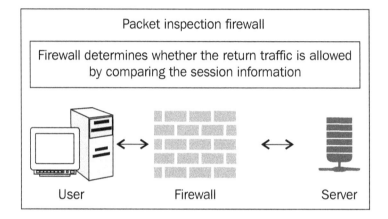

They classify and track the state of traffic by monitoring all the connection interactions until a connection is closed. They collect all the packets related to an interaction, determine their acceptability, and then release them to the network. These operate up to layer four of the OSI model. This is the transport layer.

These firewalls are a major help in thwarting **Distributed Denial of Service** (**DDOS**) attacks.

Application layer firewalls

These firewalls work on the application level of the TCP/IP stack. These address applications such as browser traffic (HTTP), telnet, or **File Transfer Protocol** (**FTP**) traffic. These firewalls are designed to intercept, examine, and drop or accept packets traveling to and from an application. As a part of their role, they are designed to drop other packets without any acknowledgment to the sender, as shown in the following image:

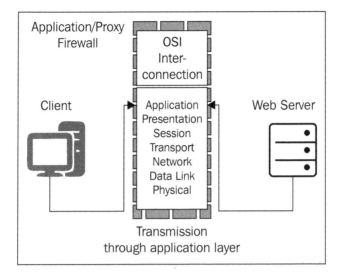

While these firewalls can be set up to inspect and intercept network packets containing Trojans and Worms, this comes at an extra latency cost, resulting in delays in packet forwarding.

Application firewalls can work by hooking into socket calls and filtering connections between the lower layers (of the OSI model) and the application layer. Firewalls that perform such a function are often called socket filters. Another role that application firewalls are involved in is managing **Network Address Translation** (**NAT**) and **Port Address Translation** (**PAT**). A key strength of application firewalls is the information that is collected in the logs.

Application firewalls come in two varieties: network-based application firewalls and host-based application firewalls. While a network-based application firewall monitors calls through the OSI stack, a host-based application firewall monitors activity through system calls. This can monitor application input and output, the system service calls made by an application, as well as the calls made from or to it.

Interpreting firewall logs

Just as we had seen earlier in the case of proxy servers, the logs collected by firewalls are a major asset to the investigator. Most firewall vendors have their own log formats that they make available to users for use. Sometimes, they have a large number of fields, which really increases the granularity of the investigation. However, most firewall logs share some common characteristics.

These include date and time. Let's look at the logs generated by a CyberRoam appliance:

Data Fields	Type	Description
Date *	date	Event date (yyyy-mm-dd).
Time*	time	Event time (hh:mm:ss).
timezone	string	Appliance timezone, for example, EST, PST, IST, and GMT.
device_name	string	Appliance model number.
device_id	string	Appliance unique identifier.
log_id	string	Unique 12 characters code comprising of the following: **Log type**, for example, 01 for firewall log. **Log component**, that is, firewall / local ACL/ DOS attack. **Log sub-type**, that is, allow/violation. **Priority**, for example, 0 for emergency. **Message ID**, for example, 00001 for traffic allowed by firewall.
log_type	string	Event type, for example, firewall event.
log_component	string	Logging component, for example, firewall rule.
log_subtype	string	Sub-type of event.
Status *	string	Ultimate status of traffic—allowed or denied.
priority	string	Severity level of traffic.
duration	integer	Durability of traffic (seconds).
firewall_rule_id	integer	Firewall rule ID, that is, firewall rule ID that is applied on the traffic.
user_name	string	Username.
user_group	string	Group ID of the user.
iap	integer	Internet access policy.
ips_policy_id	integer	IPS policy ID applied on the traffic.
appfilter_policy_id	integer	Application filter policy ID.
application	string	Application name.
in_interface	string	Interface for incoming traffic, for example, Port A. Blank for outgoing traffic.
out_interface	string	Interface for outgoing traffic, for example, Port B. Blank for incoming traffic.

Data Fields	Type	Description
src_ip*	string	Original source IP address of traffic.
src_mac	string	Original source MAC address of traffic.
src_country_code	string	Code of the country to which the source IP belongs.
dst_ip*	string	Original destination IP address of traffic.
dst_country_code	string	Code of the country to which the destination IP belongs.
Protocol*	integer	Protocol number of traffic.
src_port *	integer	Original source port of TCP and UDP traffic.
dst_port *	integer	Original destination port of TCP and UDP.
icmp_type	integer	ICMP type of ICMP traffic.
icmp_code	integer	ICMP code of ICMP traffic.
sent_pkts	integer	Total number of packets sent.
received_pkts	integer	Total number of packets received.
sent_bytes	integer	Total number of bytes sent.
recv_bytes	integer	Total number of bytes received.
trans_src_ip	integer	Translated source IP address for outgoing traffic. It is applicable only in route mode. Possible values are as follows: " ": When appliance is deployed in the Bridge mode or source IP address translation is not done. IP Address: IP address with which the original source IP address is translated.
trans_src_port	integer	Translated source port for outgoing traffic. It is applicable only in route mode. Possible values are as follows: " ": When appliance is deployed in the Bridge mode or source port translation is not done. Port: Port with which the original port is translated.
trans_dst_ip	integer	Translated destination IP address for outgoing traffic. It is applicable only in route mode. Possible values are as follows: " ": When appliance is deployed in the Bridge mode or destination IP address translation is not done. IP Address: IP address with which the original destination IP address is translated.

Data Fields	Type	Description
trans_dst_port	integer	Translated destination port for outgoing traffic. It is applicable only in route mode. Possible values are as follows: N/A: When appliance is deployed in the Bridge mode or destination port translation is not done. Port: Port with which the original port is translated.
srczonetype	string	Type of source zone, for example, LAN.
dstzonetype	string	Type of destination zone, for example, WAN.
dir_disp	string	Packet direction. Possible values are as follows: org, reply, and ""
connection_event		Event on which this log is generated.
conn_id	integer	Unique identifier of the connection.
vconn_id	integer	Connection ID of the master connection.

Now that we see all the variables involved in a log, let's see a few log entries so that we can relate to them when we work on a case:

Event: Firewall Traffic

Denied Component: Firewall Rule

Sample Log:

date=2015-08-07 time=16:27:27 timezone="GMT" device_name="CR500ia" device_id= C070123456-ABCDEF log_id=010102600002 log_type="Firewall" log_component="Firewall Rule" log_subtype="Denied" status="Deny" priority=Information duration=0 fw_rule_id=3 user_name="" user_gp="" iap=2 ips_policy_id=0 appfilter_policy_id=0 application="" in_interface="PortG.16" out_interface="PortB" src_mac=00:0d:48:0a:05:45 src_ip=172.16.16.95 src_country_code= dst_ip=192.168.5.2 dst_country_code= protocol="UDP" src_port=42288 dst_port=53 sent_pkts=0 recv_pkts=0 sent_bytes=0 recv_bytes=0 tran_src_ip= tran_src_port=0 tran_dst_ip= tran_dst_port=0 srczonetype="" dstzonetype="" dir_disp="" connid="" vconnid=""

Event: Local ACL traffic allowed

Component: Local ACL

Sample Log:

date=2015-08-07 time=14:44:57 timezone="GMT" device_name="CR500ia" device_id= C070123456-ABCDEF log_id=010301602001 log_type="Firewall" log_component="Appliance Access" log_subtype="Allowed" status="Allow" priority=Information duration=30 fw_rule_id=0 user_name="" user_gp="" iap=0 ips_policy_id=0 appfilter_policy_id=0 application="" in_interface="PortG.2" out_interface="" src_mac=00: 0:00: 0:00: 0 src_ip=172.16.16.54 src_country_code= dst_ip=192.168.52.31 dst_country_code= protocol="ICMP" icmp_type=8 icmp_code=0 sent_pkts=1 recv_pkts=1 sent_bytes=212 recv_bytes=212 tran_src_ip= Firewall Log Format tran_src_port=0 tran_dst_ip= tran_dst_port=0 srczonetype="" dstzonetype="" dir_disp="" connevent="Stop" connid="3153155488" vconnid=""

Event: Local ACL traffic denied

Component: Local ACL

Sample Log:

date=2013-08-07 time=13:25:27 timezone="IST" device_name="CR500ia" device_id=C070100126-VW717U log_id=010300602345 log_type="Firewall" log_component="Appliance Access" log_subtype="Denied" status="Deny" priority=Information duration=0 fw_rule_id=0 user_name="" user_gp="" iap=0 ips_policy_id=0 appfilter_policy_id=0 application="" in_interface="PortG.4" out_interface="" src_mac=d0:17:78:d6:4c:b0 src_ip=10.104.13.140 src_country_code= dst_ip=255.255.255.255 dst_country_code= protocol="UDP" src_port=47779 dst_port=8167 sent_pkts=0 recv_pkts=0 sent_bytes=0 recv_bytes=0 tran_src_ip= tran_src_port=0 tran_dst_ip= tran_dst_port=0 srczonetype="" dstzonetype="" dir_disp="" connid="" vconnid=""

Our networks are constantly being probed from the Internet and from an investigation perspective, it pays to look within the firewall logs for the IP addresses that are rejected. This gives us a view into what is being probed and we get an insight into what we should work at protecting.

Another thing to look out for in our firewall logs are the unsuccessful login attempts. This is a great indicator that our network is under attack and it also indicates the specific resource that is being targeted at the time.

Assuming that we have a good idea of the normal outbound traffic from our systems, our firewalls will give us a great insight into the traffic that is not characteristic. This kind of traffic may be indicative of a bot infection and highlight the servers trying to report in.

As we can see, there is a wealth of information in these firewall logs. Therefore, we must keep an eye on the evidence from firewalls as this can definitely be an asset to our network forensic investigation.

Let's move on to see what we can find from another crucial network component—routers.

Tales routers tell

On the 15th of September, 2015, the information security world was shaken by the news that a hack called SYNful knock modified the firmware of some CISCO routers. This allowed the attackers to maintain a persistent presence in the router, thereby exposing the network traffic and enabling the router to act as a listening post for the attacker.

Routers have long been the cornerstone of the Internet. The role of the router has been to connect the networks to the Internet and choose the best path so that the information arrives quickly. In fact, the global trend is that the national network infrastructures are dependent on the routers to handle the network traffic. Therefore, it stands to reason that if routers carry the world's traffic, they would also be privy to all the associated traffic logs:

What is a router?

- A router is hardware device designed to receive analyze and move incoming packets to another network.

- It interconnects two or more computer networks and forward data packets along networks.

- It also contains firmware for different networking communication protocol standards. Each network interface uses this specialized computer software to enable data packets to be forwarded from one protocol transmission system to another.

Computer   Router   Server

Seeing the kind of role that routers play, routers are often the target of attacks, especially **Denial-of-service (DoS)** or disabling the router type of attacks. Router compromise is also known where the router is used to bypass other network security components such as a firewall or an IDS.

Routers store information such as passwords and routing tables as well as information about the network blocks. This makes them intermediate targets. Compromised routers can be used as stepping stones to attack the rest of the network.

Let's take a quick look at the memory storage in routers.

While routers have two types of memory, the actual memory storage available is quite small. The first is the flash or persistent memory. This has the firmware, iOS, and relevant configuration information and is reasonably permanent. The second is the RAM. This is very volatile and the data contained in it can be completely lost if switched off. From an investigation perspective, this data can be very important as it contains the following components:

- Temporary passwords
- The current running configuration
- Statistics
- Local logs
- Scheduler
- Listening services
- ARP tables
- Dynamic routing tables
- NAT
- ACL violations

As we can see, if the router is shutdown prior to gathering all this, valuable information will be lost. However, persistent (flash memory) data will not be affected. For a successful investigation, we need to recover the volatile data on a priority basis as the first step.

In such a case, a physical connection to the router is required before we can acquire the required evidence. A laptop with appropriate cables to connect to the console port will be required. The laptop would need to have the Terminal software loaded on it to enable us to connect to the router directly rather than over the network.

Once connected we need to determine the following:

- Router current time
- Who is logged on
- Uptime since last boot
- Listening sockets (such as telnet)
- Startup configuration
- Running configuration
- IP route
- IP arp

- IP sockets
- IP NAT translations
- SNMP users and group
- Logging

The logging aspect is also very important. Once connected to the router, it is worth checking to see if buffered logging is turned on. If yes, the `show logging` command will show us the insides of the router log buffer, the level it is set to, as well as the hosts the logs are sent to. Terminal logging allows non-console sessions for viewing log entries. Syslog logging enables messages to be sent to a specified syslog server. ACL violation logging will produce a large number of interesting logs in the log buffer documenting ACL violations.

In addition to the preceding two sources of evidence (namely volatile memory and logs), the recent CISCO router hack shows that non-volatile flash memory is also vulnerable. The current hack has demonstrated that any modification in firmware remains in the persistent memory and can cause large-scale data leaks.

Summary

This chapter, though a bit long, has exposed us to three very important components of any network. As network forensic investigators, you learned about the underlying technologies and sources of evidence obtainable from proxies, firewalls, and routers. You also learned the roles they play in the big scheme of things and understood how and where the evidence resides.

We took a look at the Squid proxy server and different log formats that are prevalent for each of these components. We developed an understanding of the different fields in the log file and what each of these fields represent. We also gained an insight into the key role the routers play, the persistent and volatile memory that they have, the logs, as well as the importance of gathering information from both these memories and logs from a network forensic's perspective.

We made interesting progress and as we move on, we will study how data is smuggled through VPN tunnels in the next chapter. We will also see the different types of tunnels as well as VPN vulnerabilities.

8
Smuggling Forbidden Protocols – Network Tunneling

"Tunnels have been the refuge of many a smuggler!"

– Samir Datt

In the good old days (and even now), smugglers would need to ship foreign contraband (unauthorized products) across the borders without the border security forces or coast guard finding out. To do this, tunnels were commonly used.

The network world has startling similarities when it comes to shipping unsupported and unauthorized protocols across the network borders. This is done by the means of tunneling. In a nutshell, what a tunnel involves is encapsulating the unsupported (or unauthorized) protocol in the data portion of the IP datagram and then using the IP protocol to send it. Tunneling protocols work mostly at the fourth layer of the OSI model. This means that they replace protocols such as TCP or UDP.

Virtual private networks, or VPNs in short, completely depend on tunneling for their functioning. This chapter will cover the VPN tunnels and functional, confidential, and covert tunneling. We will look at the various tunneling protocols as well as study about the vulnerabilities of the system.

The chapter will cover the following topics:

- Understanding VPNs
- How does tunneling work?
- Types of tunneling protocols
- Various VPN vulnerabilities and logging

Understanding VPNs

Most organizations have private networks just dedicated to organizational use. The network could be a LAN, WAN, or MAN, depending upon the geographies involved and the requirements of the organization. **Virtual private networks** (**VPNs**), as the name suggests, are virtual networks that provide the private network experience for users over a public (unsecured) network — the Internet. To clarify, a VPN provides a secure tunnel to connect users outside the private network with their organizational network. VPNs use authentication and encryption for the data sent between the organization and the user outside the network boundaries:

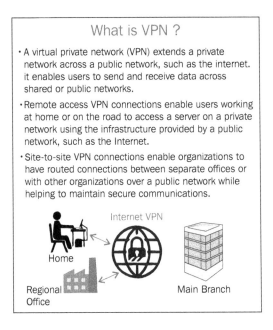

VPNs can also be used to create secure connections between two geographically different offices, such as is in the case of branch offices and the head office. VPNs can play an altogether different role. Whenever a user wishes to access certain resources and does not wish the traffic to be intercepted or the IP address to be identified, the user may use a VPN to access such resources.

Types of VPNs

VPNs fill a very important need and as a result, are fairly widespread. There are predominantly two types of VPNs, as follows:

- Remote access VPNs
- Point-to-point VPNs

Remote access VPNs

A remote access VPN is used to provide secure organizational network access to remote users over public telecommunication infrastructure such as the Internet. This involves installing a specialized client on the remote user's computer or hand-held device. This client then connects to a VPN gateway on the organizational network. The gateway first requires the remote user's device to undergo identity authentication, then it creates an encrypted network link back to the remote device. This link or tunnel allows the remote user to act as if it was present locally in this network and to reach and utilize the organization's internal network resources such as servers, printers, and so on.

Some remote access VPNs provide secure access to a single application and are designed to be application-specific (for example, SSL virtual private networks), while others provide Layer 2 access (IPSec) to the whole internal network. These typically require a tunneling protocol, such as PPTP or L2TP, running across the IPSec connection.

Remote access VPNs usually comprise two major components.

The first is the **Remote Access Server (RAS)**, also commonly known as the **Network Access Server (NAS)** (this is different from the Network Attached Storage, which is commonly associated with the NAS acronym). This NAS validates the user's credentials and allows the user to log in to the VPN. The NAS may have its own authentication process or alternatively use an authentication server present on the network to authenticate the remote user:

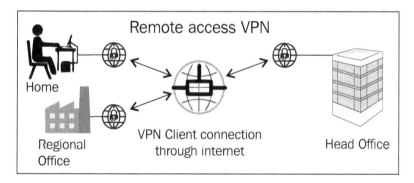

The second component is the VPN client software. The role of the VPN software is to build a tunnel to the VPN server as well as ensure the encryption of data in the tunnel. A lot of OSs have built-in VPN capabilities. External VPN tools are also available and are quite popular.

Point-to-point VPNs

Point-to-point VPNs can be between specific locations or sites (in which case, we would call it a site-to-site VPN) or between specific servers/computers such as servers in two different data centers.

In the case of a site-to-site VPN, an entire network in a particular location is connected to another network at some other location (such as a branch office) via gateway devices. No VPN clients are required to be installed on the end user computers at these locations. These computers access the network normally and all the connection requests to the other network are handled seamlessly by the gateway.

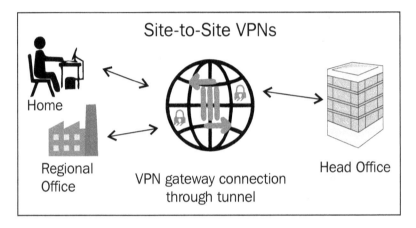

Most VPNs that connect one site to another over the Internet use IPSec. Rather than using public Internet, carrier MPLS clouds can also be used as transport. Connectivity can be Layer 2 (Virtual Private LAN Service) or Layer 3 (MPLS).

Specific computers can also be set up to communicate directly with each other via a VPN. Typically, these could be highly secure servers in geographically different data centers, where the need for security is much higher than that set up for the current network environment.

The AAA of VPNs

AAA stands for authentication, authorization, and accounting. These three are the cornerstones of secure access in a VPN environment:

- **Authentication**: This involves the authentication of a user by the means of a valid username and password. In the absence of an authentication mechanism, any one with a preconfigured VPN client has a direct entry into a secure remote network. User authentication data (usernames and passwords) may be stored on the VPN device or on a separate AAA server.

- **Authorization**: This is the second stage. At this point, the server has already authenticated the user and now moves on to determine the authorization levels of the user. This determines what the user is permitted to do.

- **Accounting**: The accounting stage is where a record of all the activity done by the user is maintained. This is the logging stage that is used extensively for security auditing, forensics, and reporting purposes.

The following image depicts the AAA concept:

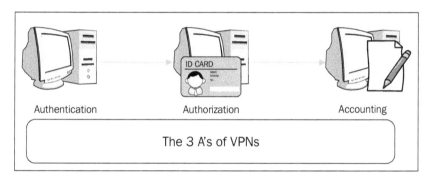

The key to VPN connectivity and security is the secure tunneling done through public networks such as the Internet. Therefore, let's move onwards to try and understand how tunneling works.

How does tunneling work?

The process of encapsulating a packet within another packet and then sending it over the network is known as tunneling.

As we are aware, every packet has a header that contains details relating to the IP version, length of the IP header, size of the IP datagram, source address, destination address, flags, and a host of other data. The header length is usually 20 bytes. The remainder portion of the packet is the data. Tunneling involves hiding unsupported or unauthorized packets within the data portion of the IP datagram. In such cases, the available space is less than what it is usually and at times, this can cause a problem in the transmitted data.

Data tunneling is often used to hide the origin of the traffic across the network. The original packet and header is encapsulated and encrypted and an additional layer 3 header is added on top. In this manner, the process of tunneling neatly hides the original source of the packet. At the destination, the trusted computer strips away the original header and determines the true source and decrypts the original header. One important thing to consider is that tunneling, by itself, does not ensure security. In the event that a packet capturing device is enabled, the data encapsulated in another packet may be visible if the packet is not encrypted.

Tunneling involves the following three different protocol types:

- **Passenger protocol**: This is the protocol that is carried in the main datagram. IP, IPX, and NetBUEI are the examples of the passenger protocols.

- **Encapsulating protocol**: This is the wrapper protocol, which means the protocol that wraps around the passenger data. The examples are IPSec, GRE, L2F, L2TP, and PPTP.

- **Carrier protocol**: This is the protocol that is used by the network for data transmission. Information travels over this protocol. IP is the main transport protocol.

The passenger protocol packet is encapsulated and at times, encrypted in the encapsulating protocol datagram. This is then put in the carrier protocol (usually IP) for transmission over the Internet. This allows safe and secure transmission of the protocols that would normally not have been transmitted over the Internet (such as NetBEUI).

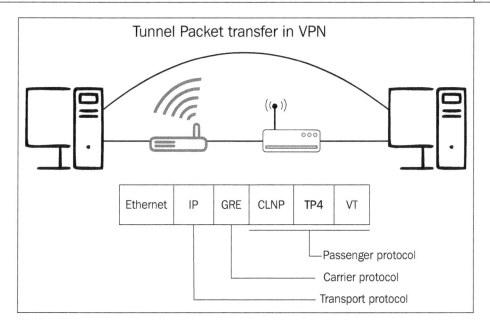

At this point, it would be useful for the investigators to note that IPSec has become quite common these days. IPSec provides security services for IP packets by encrypting traffic data. The way IPSec works in tunnel mode is to encrypt an IP packet, then encapsulate it and add a new IP header, and finally send it to the other end of the tunnel. The way various tunneling protocols work with IPSec are listed in the following sections.

SSH tunneling

SSH or Secure Shell tunneling involves the creation of an encrypted tunnel via an SSH protocol connection. SSH tunnels can be set up as an encrypted channel to transport unencrypted traffic (such as SMB−Server Message Block−protocol on Microsoft Windows machines) over the network. Tunneling, essentially, involves port forwarding. When setting up SSH tunneling, we can configure the local SSH client to forward a local port number to a specified port number on the remote machine. After setting up the SSH tunnel, a local user just needs to connect to the specified local port in order to gain secured access to the remote machine via this port. It is not necessary for the port numbers to be the same for the port forwarding to work seamlessly.

In the earlier SMB example, if we were to mount a Windows machine and access it remotely, anybody intercepting the traffic would be able to have full access to the transferred files. This is because the SMB protocol is unencrypted. However, if we were to use an SSH tunnel to route all the SMB traffic to and from the remote machine, the data would be secured by the SSH tunnel that is encrypted and the data would only be accessible to the authorized user.

SSH tunnels can also be used to bypass firewalls and proxies that are configured to monitor user activity in the organization's perimeter. In an organization that restricts direct web browsing by routing all traffic for port 80 via the proxy (from the perspective of monitoring Internet activity), a local user can access a remote SSH server in order to enable an SSH tunnel allowing port forwarding of a local port (for example, 3001) to port 80 of a remote web server. However, the important thing to note is that this is only possible if the organization policies allow outgoing connections.

An additional point of interest is the aspect of dynamic port forwarding. Some SSH clients allow dynamic port forwarding. This permits the user to create a SOCKS 4/5 proxy. Once this is done, a user can configure their application to use the more flexible SOCKS proxy server. In this case, there is no need to create an SSH tunnel to a single port on a remote server.

Types of tunneling protocols

As we have learned in the previous sections, a tunnel is a way of shipping a foreign protocol across a network that will not support it directly. Let's take a look at the different tunneling protocols and their characteristics to see how this is done.

The Point-to-Point Tunneling Protocol

Point-to-Point Tunneling Protocol is also known as PPTP. This was created by a consortium including Microsoft and other companies. PPTP is a fast protocol that, besides Windows, is also available to Linux and Mac users.

While PPTP does not have an inbuilt capability to provide traffic encryption, it relies on the **Point-to-Point Protocol** (**PPP**) to provide security measures during transmission.

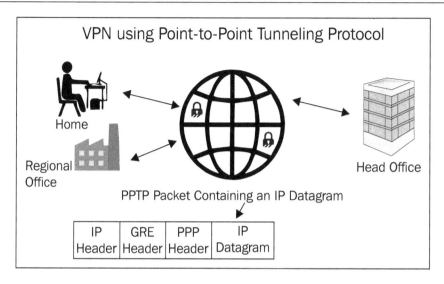

PPTP allows traffic with different protocols to be encrypted and then encapsulated in an IP datagram to be sent across an IP network such as the Internet.

PPTP encapsulates PPP frames in the IP datagrams using a modified version of **Generic Routing Encapsulation** (**GRE**). A TCP connection is used for tunnel management. The encapsulated payload can be compressed, encrypted, or both before transmission. This encapsulated PPP frame is first encrypted using the **Microsoft Point-to-Point Encryption** (**MPPE**). MPPE supports 128-bit key (this is the strongest), 56-bit key, and 40-bit key (standard) encryption schemes. A point to note is that MPPE is limited to encryption and does not have any role in the compression or expansion of data in the PPP frames that are handled by Microsoft Point-to-Point Compression.

Layer 2 Tunneling Protocol

Layer 2 Tunneling Protocol is commonly known as L2TP. This protocol was jointly developed by Microsoft and Cisco with the objective of providing data integrity along with the data confidentiality offered by the PPTP protocol. Similar to the PPTP protocol, L2TP does not provide encryption and uses PPP to do this.

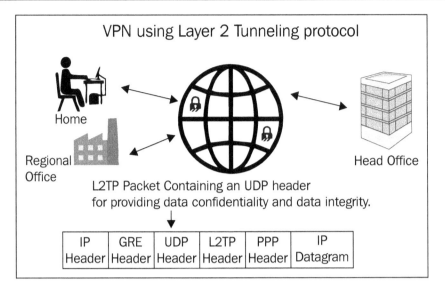

In the Microsoft implementation of L2TP, the encryption of PPP datagrams is not done with MPPE but with Internet Protocol security or IPSec. Therefore, this protocol is usually referred to as L2TP/IPSec. For L2TP/IPSec to work, both the VPN server and client need to have support for this.

L2TP/IPSec is built in most operating systems such as Windows, Linux, and Apple. It is very easy to implement.

IPSec is considered fairly secure from a security perspective and does not have any known major vulnerabilities (so far). However, Snowden, as part of his many revelations, did mention that IPSec was compromised by the NSA.

For the purposes of authentication, L2TP supports pre-shared keys or computer certificates. Computer certificate authentication requires a PKI to issue a certificate to the VPN server and all the VPN clients. The use of L2TP/IPSec provides the computer/server authentication at the IPSec-layer and user-layer authentication at the PPP layer. L2TP is encrypted using **Data Encryption Standard (DES)** or triple DES.

IPSec usage ensures data confidentiality, integrity, and authentication for VPN connections:

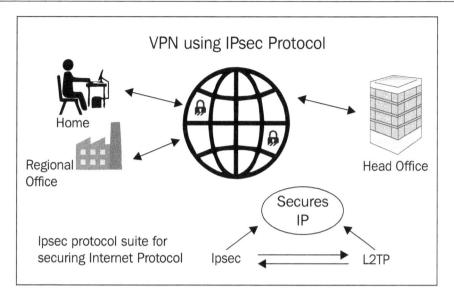

Secure Socket Tunneling Protocol

Secure Socket Tunneling Protocol is also known as SSTP. This is a new tunneling protocol that utilizes HTTPS over TCP port 443. This allows it to pass the traffic through firewalls and proxies that may be configured otherwise to block PPTP or L2TP/IPSec traffic. SSTP works by establishing a bi-directional HTTPS layer with the SSTP server. The SSTP data packets flow over this HTTPS layer.

This HTTPS layer or Secure Socket Layer performs traffic integrity checking, as well as encryption and transport-level security. SSTP is suited to remote client-access VPNs and usually does not support site-to-site VPN tunnels.

As SSTP operates over TCP transport, its performance is dependent on the availability of bandwidth over the TCP channel. In cases of bandwidth shortage, the phenomenon of TCP meltdown is common.

In all the previous three tunneling protocols, the PPP frames are carried on top of the network protocol stack. Therefore, the PPP features such as IPv4 and IPv6 negotiation, Network Access Protection, as well as authentication are common across all the three protocols.

Various VPN vulnerabilities & logging

Given the wide spread use of VPNs, extended functionality that they provide, economy of use, and their transparency to the user, it was just a matter of time before the bad guys began to target VPNs. Some of the reasons the VPNs are targeted include the following:

- Users tend to use VPNs to transmit sensitive information. This is understandable as the common belief is that VPNs are secure.

- VPNs usually have full and unrestricted access to the internal networks. Gaining access via a VPN provides full and unfettered access to the corporate networks.

- VPNs provide anonymity from IDSs if they are configured to operate outside the VPN. Any bad guy who gains access to the VPN can hide in the encrypted tunnel and not be detected by the IDS.

- VPNs are comparatively soft targets. This is because people tend to consider IPSec relatively secure and tend to spend resources hardening other network components.

So, what are the ways the VPNs can be compromised? Understanding this will help us to understand what we should look for from an investigation perspective.

To get started, let's take one more quick look at the structure of a VPN. At one end is the VPN server and at the other is the VPN client. Both of these are connected to each other using a secure tunnel. From a security perspective, the easiest points to compromise are the two end points. Usually, the VPN client is the least protected and is used in all sorts of low security areas, such as airports and free Wi-Fi zones. VPN clients are deployed in hand-held/portable devices as well. One aspect of the VPN client running on devices such as this is availability. From a bad guy's perspective, the longer they have access to a device, the higher are the chances of being able to compromise it. This may not be the case when we look at remote users using VPN clients. Conversely, the VPN server (as part of its job description) is constantly available and seeking connections. Therefore, both of the end points are likely to be subject to different types of attacks when the objective is to take advantage of their vulnerabilities.

Currently, IPSec is the most important protocol when it comes to VPNs. It is largely considered the most secure of all the VPN implementations. Unfortunately, it is also the most complex to correctly implement. Administrators with expertise and experience are required to implement IPSec effectively. The lack of such administrators leads to default configurations or misconfigurations, which contribute to a weak security posture in a surprisingly large number of cases.

One of the easiest and actually very common methods of getting unfettered access to corporate networks is by the theft of company laptops. A lot of users tend to save their VPN access credentials on their remote devices/computers, therefore, a loss of such laptop can mean the loss of data from the company's network. VPN cached credentials including data stored in the registry may be retrieved and used for malicious purposes.

Another method of gaining access to VPNs is by compromising the client or server machine by infecting the system or by a **man-in-the-middle** (**MITM**) attack. In the event the machine is infected, user credentials may be compromised and misused.

Some methods of securing such compromises are by having client **whole disk encryption** (**WDE**) in case of theft, strong firewall and virus protection to prevent client and server compromises, authentication using tokens and access control systems with user provisioning, and identity systems with the VPN administration.

Another example is forgetting to disable the VPN account of terminated employees. In 2005, this was the cause of a massive attack on Walmart's network that was breached and internal data was accessible to the ex-employee. This included payment card information. This attack lasted for a period of about 18 months and was only detected by accident (and a bit of foolishness by the attacker).

An interesting case involved an ex-employee selling off a used VPN gateway, which was found by the buyer to be still configured to access the corporate network long after the employee had left the organization.

In 2010, a high-profile vulnerability involving IPv6 and PPTP was made public. This exposed the IP address, MAC address, and computer name. More recently, in 2015, researchers from Sapienza University of Rome and Queen Mary University of London discovered security vulnerabilities in 14 popular VPN providers. It was found that some of these were exposing a user's complete browsing history. These vulnerabilities were classified as IPv6 traffic leakage and DNS hijacking.

Clientless VPN products also pose a security risk. These aggregate the data retrieved from different sites and serve it up so that it appears to be from the SSL VPN. This allows a malicious website to be also served up to the viewer while seeming to come from a single source via the SSL VPN. The bad guy could hijack a user session or capture the user's keystrokes and gain access to the VPN.

The **Internet Key Exchange (IKE) Aggressive Mode (AM)** can also cause a serious breach of information security on older clients. IPSec, when negotiating a tunnel connection, performs an exchange of information between two clients. This key exchange can happen in either the Main mode or the Aggressive mode. While the Main mode uses a six-way handshake, the Aggressive Mode uses a three-way handshake. During the AM handshake, the VPN device sends the hashed PSK in an unencrypted form. This allows an attacker to carry out an attack using tools such as L0phtcrack, psk-crack, Cain, John the Ripper, and so on.

While the previously mentioned methods of VPN compromise are, by no means, exhaustive, the key for the investigators is the logs that document all the network interactions and indicators of compromise. This helps us identify who did what, where, when, and how.

Information captured needs to include the following:

- User
- Event date and time
- Command
- Authentication status - Success/Failure
- Authorization status - Success/Failure
- Configuration changes (to detect tampering with Anti-viruses / IDS / IPS / Firewalls and so on) - as an example, the banking Trojan is known to disable firewalls
- Network addresses
- Network protocols
- Privileged access

All the investigations would require us to look at these audit trails to successfully move our network forensic investigations forward.

Summary

In this chapter, we understood the concept of virtual private networks and their role in networks. We looked at the various types of VPNs and their tunneling protocols. We also studied how, just like smugglers, VPNs are used to ship foreign protocols via tunnels into a corporate network. At the end of the chapter, we looked at the ways in which the VPNs can be compromised and consequently, further lead to the compromise of our networks.

In the next chapter, we gear up to look at how to investigate malware, which is one of the major causes of network incidents. Malware has been on an evolutionary spiral and has emerged as a potent cyber weapon used to compromise digital resources across the globe.

9
Investigating Malware – Cyber Weapons of the Internet

"Malware are the cyber weapons of the information age"

– Samir Datt

Our information age lives are driven by technology. Day in, day out, we live with technology from morning to evening. Technology drives our lives, governs our behavior, manages our finances, enables our work, facilitates our communications, and even enhances our relationships. Hence, it should not come as a surprise that technology also drives the crimes of today. A whole new industry has come up around technology-driven crimes. Organized criminals have taken to cyber crime in a big way. Even countries and states have gone in for cyber warfare. Where there is crime and war, weapons cannot be far behind. Weaponization of the Internet is a multibillion-dollar industry and malware, as we know it, is the weapon of choice.

In this chapter, we will work towards understanding malware, its different types, the various indicators of compromise, and the forensic methods of investigating malware.

We will divide our study into the following topics:

- Knowing malware
- Trends in malware evolution
- Malware types and their impact
- Understanding malware payload behavior
- Malware attack architecture
- Indicators of Compromise
- Performing malware forensics

Knowing malware

The word "mal" has its origin in Latin and means "bad" in English. "Ware", on the other hand, carries the meaning of "products". Hence, when we put these two together, we get the sense of having bad products or goods made with a bad intent.

As per NIST publication SP800-83, malware, also known as malicious code or malicious software, is meant to signify a program that is inserted (usually covertly) in a system with the intent of compromising or disrupting the confidentiality, integrity, or availability of the victim's data, applications, or operating system. Over the past few years, malware has emerged as an all encompassing term that includes all sorts of malicious programs, including viruses, worms, Trojans, rootkits, and so on.

Today, malware is considered the most significant external threat to computers and networks. Malware causes considerable losses to organizations in terms of the widespread damage caused, disruption of functioning, and huge recovery efforts required to get back to normal. Spyware is a significant subcategory of malware, which focuses on breaching user privacy. Spyware is used to monitor user activity (both online and offline); gather personal information, especially, related to online financial actions; and then, send it to criminals for subsequent misuse.

Malware objectives

In the previous chapters, we understood a number of tools used for network forensics. Just as we, the digital 007s of the network world, have our tools of trade, criminals and bad guys also have their own set of tools that they use to further their own nefarious purposes. These tools are known as malware. Though, malware comes in a wide variety, cyber criminals wish to install malware on victims' digital devices to achieve at least one of the following objectives:

- To gather and steal pertinent information (ID theft, keylogging, and so on)

- To provide remote access to the attacker to permit control of the infected/compromised computer and its resources

- To use the infected machine as a staging point to infect/investigate the rest of the network

- To use the infected machine to send out spam to the unwary

- To carry out a **denial-of-service** (**DoS**) attack by flooding the network or slowing down the connection

- To encrypt the infected disk and demand ransom to decrypt the files (ransomware)

- To remain undetected for as long as possible (turn off anti-virus and so on)

- To resist removal or enhance persistence

Malware origins

The menace of malware is growing by leaps and bounds. In fact, a recent news item from SC Magazine UK (`http://www.scmagazineuk.com/research-shows-12-new-malware-strains-discovered-every-minute/article/448978/`) mentions that 12 new malware strains are discovered every minute.

Making malware is no longer left in the realm of kids that do it for kicks. Malware manufacture, sale, and distribution is now a serious organized crime with really large amount of money riding on it. Recent reports of the money extracted for decrypting files that were encrypted by bitcoin ransomware such as **CryptoWall** and **CryptoLocker** show victims reporting losses as high as $18 million over a 14 month period (`http://www.coindesk.com/fbi-malware-victims-should-pay-bitcoin-ransoms/`).

Just like making a professionally manufactured product in any manufacturing facility, malware today is also manufactured or written to exacting specifications. This is done by talented programmers who write *exploits* to leverage *vulnerabilities* in existing software and hardware in use by the *targets* or planned victims. Malware is actually a part of a long chain of activities and helps in enabling the objectives of the attackers or cyber criminals.

The usual stages in this exercise are as follows:

- **Reconnoiter**: At this stage, the attacker carries out a preliminary recce to identify the potential targets (if using a shotgun approach, the attacker may attempt to access many, select the weakest or take a more targeted approach). This process can be manual or automated, depending on the attackers' objectives.

- **External information gathering**: At this stage, the attacker will proceed with network mapping, fingerprinting, and vulnerability identification.

- **Target penetration**: This is the usual stage where malware comes into play. This is when exploitation of the previously identified vulnerabilities takes place. Malware is usually delivered to the target via a delivery mechanism or the target is enticed to an infected site for a *drive-by* infection.

- **Privilege escalation**: This is the stage where the malware steps up its game with the objective of gaining the maximum level of privileges to the system and network.

- **Persistence**: At this stage, the malware works out means and ways of maintaining continuous access as well as preventing itself from being detected or removed. Additional backdoors are built, the network is scanned for further exploitable vulnerabilities, more root/administrator-level accounts are accessed, tracks are covered, logs are deleted, and evidence of compromise is eliminated.

A lot of these stages tend to telescope into each other. Malware authors have now moved onto bundling malware exploit kits that carry a number of different malwares, each targeted at different environments, which when bundled together, increase the possibility of identifying, compromising, and penetrating targets.

Trends in the evolution of malware

Malware has a very interesting history.

In 1949, an American scientist of Hungarian origin, John von Neumann, wrote *Theory of Self-Reproducing Automata*. In 1971, this theory formed the basis of an experiment on the creation of the first self-replicating computer program. This program was called the **Creeper** system, where it gained access to the target computers via the **Advanced Research Projects Agency Network** (**ARPANET**) and copied itself with the *I'm the creeper, catch me if you can* message.

An additional piece of interesting information about John von Neumann is that he later on went on to be a part of the Manhattan Project and helped in the design of atom bombs that ended the Second World War and directed the world towards Nuclearization.

While a nuclear war is a sure way to head towards **mutual assured destruction** (**MAD**), the cyber war of malware has just been escalating since it began. With no means of MAD or even attribution in a lot of cases, the attackers tend to get away with a lot of their activities.

Let's see how malware has evolved over the decades as represented by the following image:

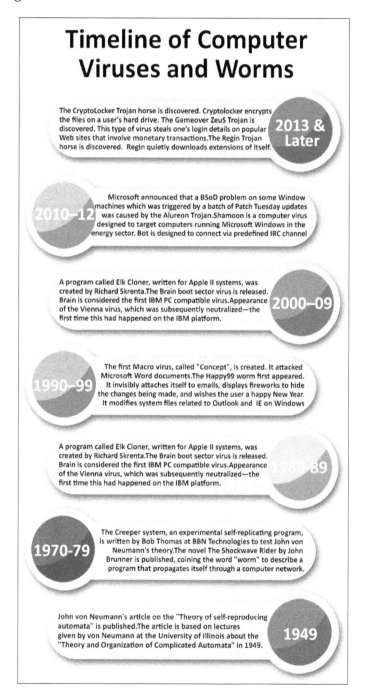

Malware types and their impact

As we had discussed earlier, malware is a malicious software that comes in a variety of names. Some of the names that it has acquired over a period of time include scamware, scareware, spamware, spyware, and so on.

Malware is all that and more. Let's take a look at the different types of malware and their impact.

Adware

Adware, as the name suggests, is an advertising-supported malware that affects your computer with the objective of serving up advertisements. This is quite a money earner for the author as they get paid based on the number of advertisements they serve up. Adware is designed to be persistent and may not be easy to remove by simply uninstalling it. Adware can be annoying at the least and it can also be part of a blended threat, as shown in the following image:

Adware reaches a victim by either downloading a supposedly useful software or visiting a site designed to affect the browser, operating system, or both.

Spyware

Spyware is a malicious software that has the objective of gathering covert information about the victim. Spyware is used to collect information related to a victim's Internet usage, e-mail and online accounts, online financial transactions, credit card and bank details, username and passwords, and so on. Spyware is becoming increasingly common in financial frauds.

Spyware can also be used to compliment Adware. This is done by monitoring the user's Internet browsing patterns and then serving up adware based on the intelligence gathered. Sometimes adware (and all malware) can masquerade as another useful program such as an anti-virus or anti-malware tool. The following pictorial representation gives us an overview of spyware:

Virus

Virus is a malicious software that is designed to replicate itself as a propagation mechanism and it usually has a payload that it delivers at a particular point of time or if certain conditions are met. A virus usually attaches itself to another piece of software and is executed every time that software is run, as shown in the following image:

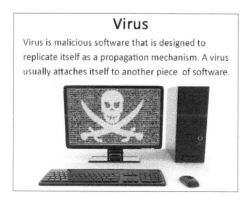

A common infection vector is the copying of software or files between multiple computers. Viruses usually modify or corrupt files on a victim's computer.

Worms

A worm, as the name suggests, is a malicious software that burrows itself in the operating system and data on a computer and then proceeds to destroy it. It has an inbuilt replication mechanism. While a virus tends to attach itself to another program, a worm is a standalone program that replicates itself and usually spreads via the network. Worms are usually the cause of some damage on a network even if it is just the consumption of bandwidth and consequent slowing of the network. The following picture shows how worms operate in a digital environment:

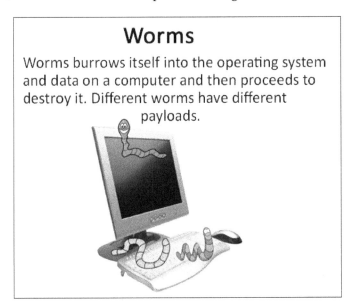

Different worms have different payloads. A payload is what a worm is designed to do other than replicate. This may involve mass mailing, data deletion, or even hard drive or file encryption based on extensions.

Worms spread by taking advantage of the vulnerabilities on the network. If the worm has been in the wild for a while, patches are usually available for the vulnerabilities it exploits and if successfully applied, its spread can be restricted. However, if it is a zero-day worm that takes advantage of an unknown/unpatched vulnerability, it can cause havoc on the network.

Trojans

It is a well-known fact that in ancient times, a hollow wooden Trojan horse, containing soldiers, masquerading as a farewell gift from the Greeks was the cause of the downfall of the city of Troy. In today's day and age, malicious software masquerading as some useful tool is known as a Trojan malware. Trojan malware can be dangerous as it has been intentionally downloaded and installed and can be identified by the user to the system as a *trusted* tool. This could result in unintended escalation of privileges.

The preferred infection vector for Trojans is via social engineering. For example, an infection occurs when a user clicks on an attachment of an e-mail assuming it to be something of use or alternatively lands up at a website with malicious code. Trojans usually have a payload. An increasingly common mode is to open a backdoor and provide access to a controller. It is not easy to detect such backdoors; however, these do result in increased traffic and more load on the processor, which shows up in the form of a compute that responds slower than normal, as shown in the following image:

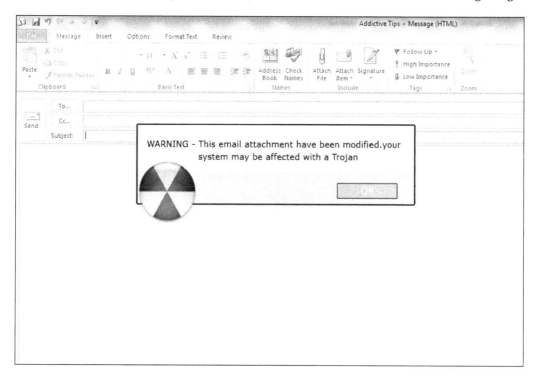

There have been a number of extremely destructive Trojans in the past and I am sure that we will see more in the future. Some of the notable ones have been NetBus, Sub7, Back Orifice, Zeus, and so on.

Rootkits

The names of the malware are really quite descriptive. As we have seen, each type of malware derives its name from some characteristic of its functioning. Along the similar lines, rootkits are actually a collection of malicious software (kits) that work at the root (or administrator) level. These could be automated or require a miscreant to obtain root privilege before installing the software. Due to the *rooted* nature of its operation, rootkits are typically hard to detect. Rootkits, once installed, establish complete control over critical functions and can prevent malware detection tools from functioning or even misreport information related to the malware presence. Rootkits can be installed in the kernel, which makes them even harder to trace and remove and may need a complete fresh reinstallation of the OS. Certain rootkits target firmware, which at times, requires a replacement of the hardware or at the very least, specialized equipment to permit a return to normalcy. A pictorial depiction of rootkits is shown as follows:

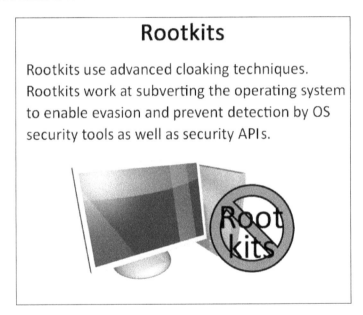

Rootkits use a number of different techniques to take control of the system. Among the most common is the exploitation of any vulnerability that exists in any component of the system under attack. This is rapidly followed by privilege escalation.

To prevent detection, rootkits use advanced cloaking techniques. Once installed and having acquired the necessary privileges, rootkits work at subverting the operating system to enable evasion and prevent detection by OS security tools as well as security APIs. This is achieved by hiding the visibility of running processes, injecting code in the operating system and modifying drivers and kernel modules. Rootkits also tend to disable event logging in order to prevent detection at a later stage.

Backdoors

Backdoors are specialized malware whose purpose is to open a backdoor into the infected system. This can be used to allow incoming requests from hackers, steal valuable data, and take complete control of the system. Backdoors can also be used to send out viruses, SPAM, or manage a network of bots. The following graphic explains backdoors in a nutshell:

Backdoors

This allows incoming requests from hackers, can be used to steal valuable data and can be used to take complete control of the system.

Keyloggers

Malware that monitors keystrokes are known as keyloggers. They log, store, and forward every key pressed on the computer on a predefined periodic basis. These keyloggers send the collected data to a specified computer, website, FTP server, online database, or e-mail address that may be hardcoded or could even be dynamically coded. These routinely capture all the data, including usernames and passwords. This data is usually captured and stored in an encrypted form. Some advanced keyloggers also send screenshots along with the key strokes captured by them. These screenshots help in correlating the key strokes captured with the context where they have been collected. Some corporate organizations employ these as a means of employee monitoring. The following graphic gives us an overview of keyloggers:

While our focus is on malware and software-based keyloggers in there, it is worthwhile to understand that hardware-based keyloggers are also available. These can be small USB-based devices or flow-through connectors through which the keyboards are connected. These can be both PS2 or USB types.

Ransomware

Ransomware is a straightforward extortion tool. This is a malicious software designed to encrypt your data and then demand a ransom for it. The encryption used these days is RSA-2048 and it is strong enough to prevent users from breaking it in any reasonable amount of time and this forces them to pay the ransom or forget about the data altogether. The payment mode is via Bitcoin or other digital currency and the payment is made via dedicated servers hosted in the **Deep Web**.

Security researchers had examined the earlier versions of Ransomware, such as CryptoLocker and CryptoWall, and had determined that these worked by encrypting a copy of the original file and then deleting the original. As the original file was deleted, victims could actually undelete the original files with the help of data recovery software and in the bargain, avoid paying the extortionists.

As soon as the malware authors realized this, they changed their approach. Not only did they begin to wipe the deleted files, they also added the threat of exposing the contents of the encrypted files in public. This dramatically increased their payment rates and they are rumored to have made over tens of millions of dollars from the payments made by the victims. The following graphic gives us an overview of what ransomware is about:

The usual infection vector for ransomware, such as CryptoWall, is by e-mail attachments. E-mails with enticing subjects are sent, containing files with the zip extension as attachments that, in reality, contain compromised executables disguised as PDF files. Some of these malware can infect files in network shares as well, allowing the infection to spread across the network.

Browser hijackers

Another dangerous variant of malware are browser hijackers. A browser hijacker takes over the browser and directs search activities to the websites that it wants the user to visit. This could be with the objective of making money from your surfing or redirecting the browser to fraudulent websites. This can be a cause of major concern, especially, when using a hijacked browser to carry out online financial transactions. A pictorial depiction of browser hijackers is shown as follows:

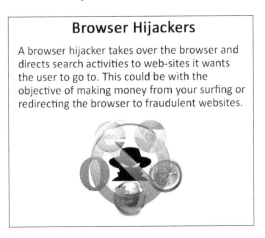

Browser Hijackers

A browser hijacker takes over the browser and directs search activities to web-sites it wants the user to go to. This could be with the objective of making money from your surfing or redirecting the browser to fraudulent websites.

Botnets

Remember the old B-grade movies with an army of zombies that would go on to do their master's bidding; botnets follow the same principal, as shown in the following image:

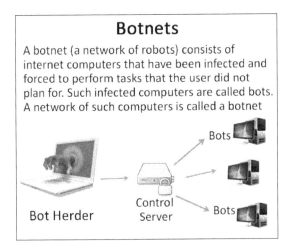

Botnets

A botnet (a network of robots) consists of internet computers that have been infected and forced to perform tasks that the user did not plan for. Such infected computers are called bots. A network of such computers is called a botnet

Bots

Bot Herder

Control Server

Bots

A botnet (a network of robots) consists of Internet computers that have been infected and forced to perform tasks that the user did not plan. Such infected computers are called bots. A network of such computers is called a botnet and the computer controlling a number of such bots is called a bot herder. A group of bot herders can report to a command and control center. The owner of a botnet can utilize their network in a number of ways. Botnets can be used to propagate infections, send out spam, carry out denial-of-service attacks, and so on. It is fairly common for botnets to be rented out or outright sold in the underground community.

Understanding malware payload behavior

Every malware out there in the jungle has a job to do. Whether it is to choke up your network or steal your money, malware is designed with an objective. This objective is known as its payload. This is the damage the malware causes to our systems or network. From a network forensic investigation perspective, it is very important for us to understand what the payload of the malware is. This helps us in identifying the extent of damage caused by the malware and figuring out how to contain, counter, or prevent the damage caused.

These payloads can be any of the following:

- Destructive
- Theft of identity
- Espionage
- Financial fraud
- Theft of data
- Misuse of resources

Let's take a brief look at each of these.

Destructive

While most payloads are destructive in one way or another, some malware specialize in carrying out focused destructive activity.

In a number of cases, destructive payloads can be easy to identify and can include crashing the infected system or device. This could also involve data corruption, modification or deletion of files, even the formatting of media, and destruction of all contents.

Some malware are designed to spread themselves across the network. Other than the self-propagation angle, this can cause a major degradation in the network's performance.

Malware has also been known to destroy hardware and make computers totally non-functional. One such early computer killer was the CIH virus that affected the BIOS on certain motherboards.

Identity theft

A very common objective of malware is identity theft. Malicious spyware monitors all the activity with the intention of grabbing information related to your identity.

The malware focuses stealing information related to the following:

- Usernames and passwords
- Credit and debit card information
- Online bank accounts
- Details of e-mail accounts and banks linked with them
- Social security numbers
- Other identity documents
- Address book information including email addresses
- Other **personally identifiable information (PII)**

Espionage

Malware has been employed at the forefront of espionage by both good and bad guys. Where state players have used malware to gather information on friends and foes alike, criminals have successfully used malware for the purposes of gathering information on potential targets. Malware has also been successfully employed to conduct industrial espionage.

In fact, malicious software such as Dino and Regin are indicative of the sophistication of the cyber weapons that have been developed for the purpose of espionage. The structure of these malware displays a degree of customizability, which allows the controllers to use them for mass surveillance and targeted spying.

The degree of technical competence and sophistication that these weapons show are indicative of the considerable resources expended on their development. The expense of building such formidable cyber weapons seems to indicate the involvement of state-level actors.

As a digital 007, it becomes very important for us to understand, detect, and identify espionage malware and its actions.

Financial fraud

A common piece of investigative wisdom in the forensics industry is *follow the money*. Unfortunately, this is exactly what cyber criminals like to do. Some very sophisticated malware is targeted towards electronic financial transactions as well as extracting funds with electronic blackmail.

A fairly common use is identifying people in international trade and monitoring their interactions with buyers or suppliers. As soon as the goods are shipped, cyber criminals step in and while impersonating the shipper, ask the buyer to deposit the due funds in another account. Once the money is transferred, the funds are quickly withdrawn or moved so that the money cannot be easily traced or recovered.

A currently prevalent malware specializes in encrypting data on systems and then demands a ransom for decrypting it. In case the ransom is not paid, the criminals threaten to leak the decrypted data on the Web. While people may be able to put up with the loss of their data, they are less likely to accept the idea of having their confidential data suddenly appearing online.

Theft of data

If there is one thing that is common across the board, it is data theft. In most cases of malware use (except some of the ones earlier mentioned), monetization of the malware happens in conjunction with data theft. Some malware focus on user credentials and financial details, some focus on images and videos, and others harvest documents and communications. Theft of trade secrets is also fairly common.

Misuse of resources

Most malware tends to establish itself in a compromised system and then moves on to the (mis)use the resources that are available for the system. Malware can assimilate a computer as part of a botnet. It can be used to automate spam or carry out distributed denial-of-service attacks. Compromised computers can also be used for mining crypto currencies such as Bitcoin. Such computers are also used to attack, infect, or recruit other computers or devices for the criminal's nefarious purposes. They have also been known to be used for spying, surveillance, and stalking of targets.

Malware attack architecture

Let's take a look at the following five pillars (stages) in the architecture of a malware attack:

1. **Entry Stage**: This is the point from where the malware attempts to enter the victim's system. This could be done via a drive by downloading or clicking a link in an e-mail, which could result in a browser hijack that directs the victim to where the attacker wants them to go.

2. **Distribution Stage**: The moment the victim connects to a malicious website, the site directs the victim seamlessly to a **Traffic Distribution Server (TDS)**. This determines the victim's OS and browser. A TDS can be quite sophisticated and can filter out connection requests based on the browser type, OS, IP addresses, and other criteria. At this stage, the TDS can be set to drop or redirect requests to decoy sites from known IP addresses of security researchers, antivirus, or malware firms. These IP addresses that meet the preset criteria are directed to the third stage.

3. **Exploit Stage**: At this stage, the attacker's objectives are to gain undetected access to the victim's computer. Based on the data gleaned about the victim's environment, the exploit kit will identify a vulnerability in the browser or browser plugins and direct the victim to a server running the specific exploit required to compromise their machine and gain a foothold in the system.

4. **Infection Stage**: This is the stage where the malicious payload is downloaded to the victim's computer and the system is infected.

5. **Execution Stage**: This is the stage where the criminals tend to take advantage of the compromised or exploited system. During this stage, the malware may call home and establish a connection to exfiltrate sensitive data or act as part of a botnet. It may even encrypt a victim's data and attempt to extort money to decrypt it.

Indicators of Compromise

Indicators of Compromise (**IOC**) as they are commonly known are the symptoms that confirm the presence of the malware malady. Essentially, from a network forensics' perspective, these are artifacts (or a remnant from an intrusion) that, when discovered on a system or network, indicate a compromise with a high degree of confidence. There are malware-specific IOC and specialized tools such as **YARA** (`http://plusvic.github.io/yara/`) that help in identifying the existence of malware based on searches for these IOC.

Typically, IOC include known rogue IP addresses, virus signatures, MD5 hashes of malware, known bad URLs or domain names, and so on.

To promote standardization, a number of open frameworks are available. However, no framework can claim to be the de facto standard. The two most important frameworks are as follows:

- **Open IOC**: This stands for **Open Indicators of Compromise**. This framework is promoted by **Mandiant** and is available at `http://www.openioc.org/`. This is a simple XML framework built with the objective of documenting and characterizing intrusion artifacts located on a host or a network.

- **CybOX™**: This stands for **Cyber Observable eXpression**. CybOX is a US **Department of Homeland Security (DHS)** led effort. CybOX also uses XML schema to describe cyber observables. CybOX is available at `https://cyboxproject.github.io/`.

Indicators of compromise can include the following components:

- E-mails from a specific IP address
- Network traffic to a specific IP address
- Registry key creation
- File deletion
- Known HTTP Get request received
- File found to match with a known MD5 hash
- Data sent to an address on a socket
- A found mutex
- Application-specific logs show communications on specific ports
- A known file's MD5 hash value has changed
- Known bad URLs or domains are detected
- The configuration of a service has changed
- A remote thread has been created

IOC, once identified, can be used to provide very effective inputs for IDS and IPS and can also be used to configure firewall rules. Therefore, any incident response activity that is planned should definitely proceed beyond the remediation stage so that the IOCs can be identified and fed back into the prevention and detection infrastructure in order to avoid the organization suffering a repeat attack.

Performing malware forensics

Now that we have the fundamentals in place, it is important to understand that malware forensics is different from malware analysis. Malware analysis involves capturing a sample of the malware and performing a static or dynamic analysis on it. Here, the compiled and obfuscated code is reversed in order to try and determine what the malware was programmed to do.

Malware forensics, on other hand, attempts to locate and examine the forensic artifacts that exist on system media, RAM, and network to help answer whether the system was compromised, how was it done, what was the infection vector, which particular malware was involved, what data is exfiltrated, and so on.

In the previous section, we looked at the IOC and how they help in identifying whether a system or network has been compromised. While this helps in cases where the compromise has been caused by known malware; for zero day or yet unknown malware or its variants, a malware forensic investigation needs to be launched.

The first indicator of a malware infection is some kind of anomalous behavior. The moment this is reported, an alert administrator gets the system checked with an updated malware detection program such as malware bytes or tools such as YARA with the known IOCs. In the event the behavior persists and no positive detection occurs, it becomes imperative to perform an in-depth malware forensic investigation.

The key element to remember when we perform forensics on a malware-affected machine is to look and acquire all the available data in reducing order of volatility. This means that we need to look at grabbing RAM, all the relevant network logs, as well as an image of the hard drive. Further, we need to closely monitor all the traffic to and from the affected system.

Let's take a look at the process that we need to follow in order to conduct an effective investigation:

- Examine the **Master Boot Record** (**MBR**): This is usually the first sector of a hard drive and has the size of 512 bytes. In the constant fight between malware and anti-malware, the struggle is to ensure who loads up first. In the event the malware makes it first, it can prevent the anti-malware from detecting it in anyway. This is where the MBR comes into play. Whenever a computer boots up, the first piece of code that gets executed is the boot code in this sector. If the malware manages to modify this to its benefit, anti-malware will fail in its task and the malware will remain resident at all times. In this case, it helps if we have a copy of the expected baselined MBR.

- ID the operating system: Once this has been adequately done, the service packs and patches identified, then it becomes easy to download the known file hashes (from **National Institute of Standards and Technology (NIST)/ Hashkeeper**) to enable the investigator to eliminate known good files from the investigation. Conversely, it becomes really easy to identify files whose MD5 hashes are different from what they should be and these could be the potentially infected or modified files.

- Examine the RAM: If we have grabbed the volatile memory as discussed in the earlier chapters, we should proceed to examine the system RAM image in an offline manner. Alternatively, a live RAM analysis can be performed; however, it should be noted that this is at the risk of compromising the volatile data as every bit of activity that we perform on a system impacts the volatile memory. Volatile memory forensics is actually a vast standalone field related to digital forensics; however, from our understanding perspective, we will look at it in a simplified manner. An examination of the volatile memory can reveal the following:

  - Currently running processes (malware active in the RAM)
  - Hidden processes
  - Recently terminated processes
  - Open files (for example, files being accessed by the malware)
  - Registry handles being accessed
  - Network connections (volatile memory has more reliable information than the one obtained by running commands, such as **netstat** whose output may have been compromised by the malware)
  - Listening ports
  - Cryptographic keys and passwords
  - Whole files
  - File fragments
  - Keyword searchable unencrypted content
  - Hidden data
  - Malicious code (fileless malware)

- Examine and hash files on disk: Volatile memory analysis shows us files that are in use or opened by the malware. This leads us to locating them on disk and examining them in great detail. This is greatly useful in identifying where the malware is collecting the data for exfiltration. Files identified as in use by the malware can be hashed and the suspicious files can be sent to online malware identification portals, such as **VirusTotal**, and hash values can be checked with **National Software Reference Library (NSRL)** at `http://www.hashsets.com/nsrl/search/`.

- Examine the registry: Look in the autostart locations, any program in multiple autostart locations should be a suspect. Malware tends to identify and place itself or its different variants in multiple autostart locations with the objective of increasing its persistence.

- Examine the programs run on the system: Identify what each program does and ask are the programs for performing a legitimate task? Unidentified programs need looking into in more detail.

- Examine the system logs: Look for things that look out of place. Identify outgoing connections.

- Examine Web browsing history: This could help in identifying whether the user has visited known compromised sites as well as identify locations from where a drive by the download has occurred.

- Examine file artifacts: Especially in the downloads and temporary folders, this may help in identifying the malware entry point. Also look for deleted files; malware may delete files that it no longer needs just to cover its tracks.

- Build a timeline: Plot all the activities gleaned from file dates, e-mails, web visits, cookies, logs and so on to try and build a sequence of events. Files that appear on your timeline within the period that you suspect the system was compromised definitely require a second look.

- Re-examine everything.

Once this is done, it is worth loading the allegedly compromised system in a virtual environment and examining all the activities performed by it. Its interaction with the network and the consequent changes in the previously baselined system will definitely be noteworthy and a further forensic examination along the previous lines could be conducted in order to gather more information about the malware and its activities.

Once the malware and its IOC have been determined, the IOCs can be added to various perimeter devices in order to prevent the recurrence of the malware on the network.

Malware insight – Gameover Zeus Trojan

The Gameover Zeus Trojan has been one of the most successful malware of all time. Like most malware, it all begins with an innocuous spam e-mail, which leads to an infection that, in turn, results in an account takeover, followed by the fraud. The money is transferred out of the bank account and to prevent its timely discovery, the bank or financial institution is subjected to a **distributed denial-of-service (DDoS)** attack. This attack causes all the security resources of the bank to be focused on tackling the DDoS and it also allows the attackers to fill the logs with so much DDoS-related data that the investigators are likely to miss or altogether lose the information relating to the financial theft. In the meantime, the money is withdrawn and effectively laundered.

Zeus began its career as a malware kit in 2005 and Zeus version 2 was launched in 2009. However, in 2011, the Zeus source code was made public and some really talented software programmers went on to refine it into a number of variants. One of the variants added the **peer-to-peer (P2P)** protocol and Gameover Zeus was born. Prior to this, there were centralized command and control servers and this made them the targets of law enforcement and anti-malware researchers.

Sophisticated peer-to-peer capabilities have really empowered the Zeus malware, decentralizing the command and control structure as well as helping in creating a botnet with the infected computers aware of nearby peers, with daily configuration updates, and weekly binary updates via the command and control channels. This lack of a single point of failure makes Gameover Zeus botnet very resilient.

P2P Zeus or Gameover Zeus is a malware targeting bank credentials and is capable of causing considerable financial losses. It harvests banking information, infects systems to join the botnet, sends out spam, is also known to deliver other malware such as CryptoLocker, and can participate in DDoS attacks. It modifies the registry and infects the `explorer.exe` and other processes. Once resident in memory, it stays dormant until a web page belonging to a financial institution is accessed, where it injects additional fields and pop-ups to steal user credentials.

Forensic artifacts left by the Gameover Zeus malware include information in the volatile memory, system logs, as well as system registry.

An example of a forensic artifact that can be found in the case of this malware is a modification in the following registry key causing the disabling of the firewall:

```
HKLM\System\Controlset002\Services\SharedAccess\Parameters\
FirewallPolicy\StandardProfile\EnableFirewall
```

The malware sets the value to `0`, disabling the firewall and reducing the chances of its detection.

Summary

This chapter focused on building our understanding of malware, what it is, how it works, what is the kind of damage it can do is, as well as how to go about identifying it. You learned about the IOC and understood how to about identifying compromised systems and networks. You also learned about the process of malware forensics and the different steps that we follow in the investigation along with their relevance.

Moving forward in our journey of understanding network forensics, we will look at how to put our knowledge that we gained so far to good use and work together to solve the case in the next chapter.

10
Closing the Deal – Solving the Case

"The end game is what really counts!"

– Samir Datt

Our journey, so far, has been an interesting one. As we traversed this ocean of network forensics, we stopped at numerous stops and islands on the way to enhance our understanding of the environment. These stops have helped us understand the various tools, technologies, and techniques that are required to conduct a network forensic investigation. We have seen the use of memory forensics that allow us to create images of RAM contents, how packet sniffers allow us to grab network data, and also how various intrusion detection and prevention servers play a role in the defense of the network. An analysis of the logs generated by proxies, firewalls, and intrusion detection and prevention systems have helped us gain an insight into networks, their behavior, and the various forensic artifacts left behind for us to find as evidence of malicious activity. We have also studied about malicious software and its various kinds and how malware affects our systems and the various steps involved in its investigations. As our travel across the ocean comes to an end, we need to stitch our knowledge together to form a map of our journey through network forensics and see how we can put all this knowledge to good use in an integrated manner.

In this final chapter, we will cover the finer aspects and provide the finishing touches to successfully take up, handle, investigate, and close a network forensics case.

Now it's time for all the Network 007s to take this final journey together through our network to learn the *end game*. That's what really counts!

We will solve our case according to the following steps:

- Revisiting the TAARA investigation methodology
- Triggering the case
- Acquiring the information and evidence
- Analyzing the collected data – digging deep
- Reporting the case
- Action for the future
- The future of network forensics

Revisiting the TAARA investigation methodology

Let's do a quick review of the TAARA network forensics and incident response methodology.

As we learned in *Chapter 1, Becoming Network 007s*, TAARA stands for the following:

- **Trigger**: This is the event that leads to an investigation.
- **Acquire**: This is the process that is set in motion by the trigger; this is predefined as part of the incident response plan and involves identifying, acquiring, and collecting information and evidence relating to the incident. This includes getting information related to the triggers, reasons for suspecting an incident, and identifying and acquiring sources of evidence for subsequent analysis.
- **Analysis**: All the evidence that is collected is now collated, correlated, and analyzed. The sequence of events is identified. The pertinent questions relating to whether the incident actually occurred or not; if it did, what exactly happened, how it happened, who was involved, what is the extent of the compromise, and so on are answered.
- **Report**: Based on the preceding analysis, a report is produced before the stakeholders to determine the next course of action.
- **Action**: The action recommended in the report is usually implemented during this stage.

The following image gives us an overview of the network forensics investigative methodology, TAARA:

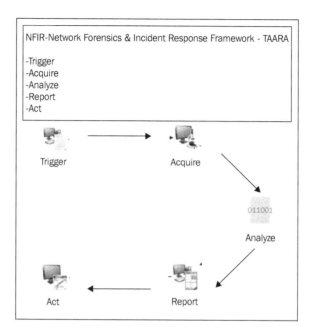

Triggering the case

A fairly large multilocational organization implemented a **Call Data Analysis & Management System**, or **CDAMS** in short, (this is a telephone log data analysis solution.). As a part of the setup process, the team of implementation consultants were requested to ingest and analyze a very large volume of calls received by the in-house IT help-desk. The year long data of call logs from the existing organization-wide **electronic private automatic branch exchanges** (**EPABX**) system were ingested by the system. Calls were filtered on the basis of call direction and destination (incoming calls to the IT help-desk) and were geolocated as well as classified based on the department. A preliminary look showed the following interesting trends:

- Calls from some cellular numbers (similar to the series owned by the company in particular geographies) at odd hours from a senior personnel
- Calls from **Computerized Numerical Control** (**CNC**) manufacturing/ machine departments requesting assistance relating to performance issues of their systems due to unidentified reasons
- Calls from foreign countries where the organization did not have operations
- Calls from corporate HQ at out-of-office hours
- Repeated calls from a few specific users at intervals of every two hours or so

While most calls signify just another day in the life of an IT help-desk technician, an in-depth analysis of the calls seemed to signify that something was amiss.

All of the preceding incidences were examined in more detail. Some were found to relate to requesting a password reset that turned out to be social engineering attempts, others related to persistent infections, as well as ongoing attacks; the CNC department had open-USB access as a functional requirement and this led to the proliferation of malware and expensive downtime.

Once these patterns were identified, it became quite easy to take preventive actions by putting external social engineering numbers and extensions requesting password resets the out-of-office hours on telephone watch lists. Other telephone patterns were correlated with security incidents and these were identified as early **Indicators of Compromise** (**IOC**). All in all, the introduction of CDAMS added a brand new dimension to network forensic investigations, as well as acted as an early warning system based on the behavioral analysis.

The story illustrates how different sources of information can act as a trigger leading to a full-fledged network forensic investigation. This could also be based on rules implemented in various perimeter security devices such as firewalls, **intrusion detection system** (**IDS**), and **intrusion prevention system** (**IPS**).

Some triggers are enumerated in the following:

- **Multiple outbound connections**: Multiple outbound connections from an internal host in a short span of time could indicate a compromised host being used to attack the external systems. An example for this would be a compromised corporate computer mass mailing unsolicited e-mails with malicious content as illustrated in the following image:

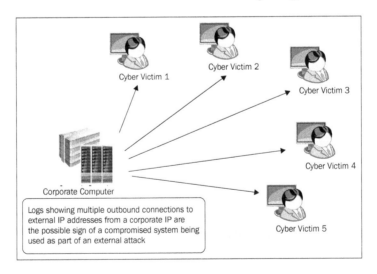

- **Communications with block listed malicious IP addresses or URLs**: As the malware economy booms, the number of URLs and IP addresses serving up malicious software is on the rise. Any internal host communicating with a known malicious IP address or URL would be a definite cause of concern to any system administrator. To enable organizations in order to block access to such malicious websites and URLs, a number of organizations constantly maintain and publish block lists. Some of these are as shown in the following:

  ° Arbor Networks: `https://atlas.arbor.net/`

  ° Clean MX database: `http://support.clean-mx.de/clean-mx/viruses`

  ° Malc0de Database: `http://malc0de.com/database/`

  ° Malware Domain Blocklist: `http://www.malwaredomains.com/wordpress/?page_id=66`

  ° FireHOL IP lists: `http://iplists.firehol.org/`

  ° OpenPhish: `http://openphish.com/`

  ° Scumware: `http://www.scumware.org/`

  ° MalwareURL List: `http://www.malwareurl.com/`

Communications between corporate networks and the outside world are depicted in the following image:

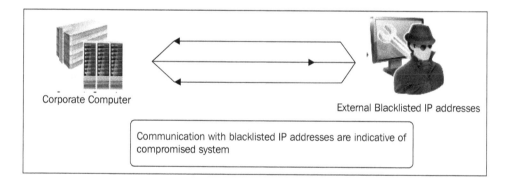

These communications could be directed inward or outward. IP addresses and URLs that serve up malware are subjected to constant surveillance and take-down operations. Therefore, these lists are dynamic in nature and need to be constantly updated in order to ensure an organization's defenses are up-to-date.

- **Standard services using non-standard ports**: Communication with external IP addresses using non-standard ports is a red flag and could be indicative of compromised systems. For example, FTP is a protocol that normally correlates to ports 20 and 21. In the event we come across entries in our logs relating to FTP usage on higher numbered ports (that which we are not aware of), there is a strong possibility that our system has been compromised as given in the following image:

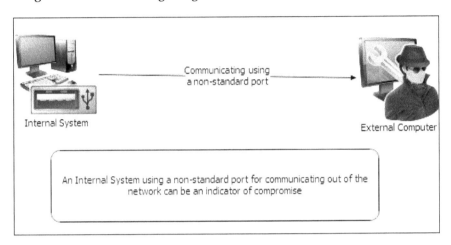

- **Lateral movement of data**: Excessive data transfer to a specific system from across the enterprise is another good IOC. Any collection of data in an obscure location of the network can signal a planned exfiltration of data after the compromise. Indications of this occurring may include the out-of-hours data transfer to a system that is divergent from the normal operational practices, excessive use of network resources, the presence of data in locations where it is not supposed to be, and so on. The way **Advanced Package Tools (APTs)** work is by gaining access to the network, identifying the digital assets of interest, lateral movement of these assets, collecting the digital assets in one place, building manageable archive segments, encrypting them, and finally exfiltrating them. In the end, these archives on the victim's networks are deleted to cover the tracks and increase persistence. Exfiltration can be a complex process as it involves uploading large volumes of data without the knowledge of the victim or detection by the victim's perimeter defenses. In cases involving internal complicity, the exfiltration may happen by something as simple as carrying the data out on an external hard drive; while in cases involving remote action, exfiltration could follow more complex paths. Cases where the exfiltrated data has been disguised as normal HTTP or HTTPS traffic are common. More exotic methods such as disguising the exfiltrated data as videos and uploading them to the cloud (onto video-sharing sites) have also been observed as shown in the following image:

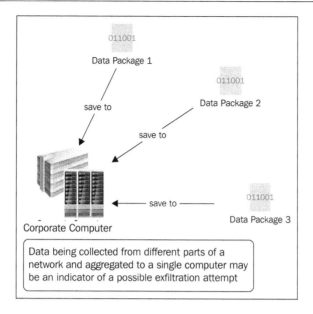

- **Multiple inbound connections**: Multiple inbound connections simultaneously sending requests to a specific network resource could be indicative of an attack in progress. If the logs indicate an abnormal number of requests (such as pings), there is a strong possibility that an attempt is being made to overwhelm the available network resources and a denial-of-service attack is in progress, as shown in the following image:

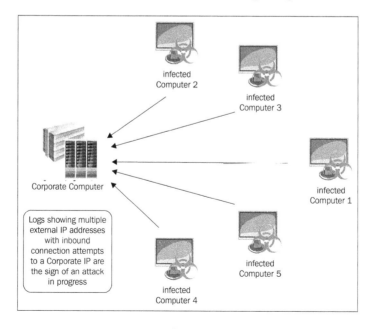

- **Multiple logins**: Multiple logins from different locations to the same or different resources at the same time may indicate a case of compromised credentials. It is fairly common for attackers to rapidly exploit the compromised credentials to gain maximum mileage possible in the shortest possible time. This results in multiple login attempts at different organizational resources to help in determining the extent of the access available. These credentials may also have been sold online and could be used by a multitude of people for different nefarious purposes, as shown in the following image:

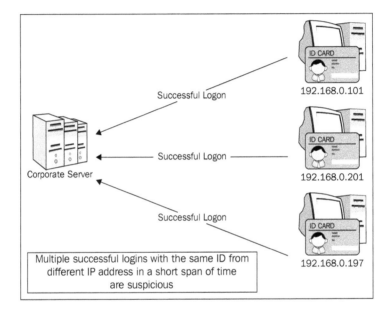

As we can see, there are a large number of known and previously unknown actions that may trigger an investigation. It usually starts with a user complaining of strange system behavior, including slow access and can continue in an upward spiral.

Let's take a look at the case that we are required to investigate.

Trigger of the case

One fine Monday morning, an organization was hit by a ransom demand. An e-mail, sent directly to the CEO, threatened the exposure of a very large volume of company's confidential information on the Web unless a large sum was transferred to a specified Bitcoin wallet. Some very sensitive sample data was attached to the e-mail to lend credence to the threat. Furthermore, recent media coverage had brought the subject of the companies being hit by ransomware to the forefront of the CEO's attention.

The CEO was thoroughly shaken and did not know whom to call. Just the idea that the confidential information could appear on the Web was enough to cause major distress. He could imagine the negative publicity, fall in the share prices, loss of customer confidence, layoffs, government intervention, and other repercussions that would follow such event.

After much deliberation, he called in the CFO, who in turn called in the CSO and CISO to discuss this issue in detail. A lot of thought and discussions later, it was decided to get in a trusted key InfoSec Team member with network forensics skills to identify where the leak occurred from and contain such exposures further. The team member was required to keep the information to himself and conduct the investigation as confidentially as possible. A cover story was created to make the investigation seem like a routine audit.

The investigator was charged with the following brief:

- Keep the investigation absolutely confidential; even the cover story was to be communicated on a need-to-know basis.
- Gather information about the breach and determine its extent — did the *datanapper* actually have all the data that they claimed to have?
- Find out how the breach occurred.
- Were the insiders involved?
- Suggest controls to prevent a repetition of the incident.
- All of this was to be done by *yesterday* (a sad fact of a network forensic investigator's life is that all jobs need to be done by yesterday).

Acquiring the information and evidence

The stage is set, the objectives are clear, it is time for us to get started. As mentioned in the earlier chapters, we needed to have a plan in place; now is the time the plan goes in to action.

However, before we begin, we need to lay a strong emphasis on the way we go about acquiring the information and evidence. A tiny slip up in the way we handle this can have widespread ramifications. Therefore, we need to focus on how to handle this stage.

Important handling guidelines

As you have learned in the earlier chapters, digital evidence is extremely fragile. In fact, just like medicines, digital evidence comes with a expiration date. The impermanence of data in memory, periodicity of log rotation, volatile storage, degradation of data on media, and the malware itself contribute to the significant loss of valuable evidence unless it is gathered, stored, and handled with due care.

All the investigators need to consider the following points:

- All actions that are performed should be in the purview of the law
- All actions that are performed should be in the purview of company policy
- An attempt should be made to gather all the information related to an incident before starting the evidence-gathering process, this enables a better understanding of the case and helps the investigator to document the possible sources of evidence
- The process of evidence gathering should not, in itself, alter the evidence in any way
- All the evidence that is gathered should be an authenticated copy of the original
- Separate secure storage for the gathered evidence should be made available to ensure integrity and chain of custody
- An emphasis should be made in properly documenting the whole process in a manner that can stand up in a court of law if required

For the purpose of the rest of the chapter, we will assume that our investigating teams took all the necessary precautions while pursuing the case. We also emphasize that all the policies and procedures are adhered to while accessing evidential data.

Gathering information and acquiring the evidence

The first part of the acquisition stage involves gathering all the information related to the case.

The beginning of the investigation involves a study of the trigger to determine the next course of action.

In our case, the e-mail to the CEO was the trigger. Therefore, the e-mail was the first bit of information that was examined to kick off the investigation.

A preliminary discussion with the CXO team as well as a detailed look at the e-mail headers brought the following interesting facts to light:

- The CEO's direct e-mail ID was not known outside the organization. In fact, all the mails sent to the CEO would actually land at his assistant's desk and she would filter and then forward very few critical mails. Therefore, a direct e-mail from a miscreant demanding ransom came as a shock. This seemed to indicate a very high level of intrusion into the corporate systems and/or insider involvement.

- The e-mail under examination was sent with an attachment that contained the sensitive data sample. This was in the form of a ZIP file, which had a size that was about 19 MB. The e-mail system was configured to reject all the files over 20 MB. This could be a coincidence or consequence of an in-depth understanding of the corporate e-mail system. It was the investigator's job to prove or disprove the coincidence.

- The ZIP file contained three confidential files, each of which the CXO team explained was sourced from different systems in the organization. It was also emphasized that the knowledge of the existence of these files was very restricted and known only to a few employees that had actually worked on the project. None of the separate teams were aware of the existence of the other two files, except the members of the leadership team present in the room.

- A preliminary examination of the e-mail headers showed that the mail had originated from the **Tor** mail. A visit to the Web showed that this service runs over the encrypted and anonymous Tor network and requires a Tor browser to access it. This is used by people who wish to communicate over e-mails in an anonymous manner on the Web.

- Other details, such as email content, date and time, time zones, header IDs, and so on were noted in the e-mail.

- The e-mail content mentioned that the hacker had over 10 GB of data and would expose it unless the ransom was paid.

- The latest versions of the documents were compared with the contents in the ZIP file and it was determined that the files in the ZIP were not more than a couple of days old. This was cross verified by the date and time of the files in the ZIP.

The following image depicts the header of a ZIP file. As seen, the date and time of the ZIP file modification are stored in the header. This usually depicts when the ZIP file was modified in order to add or remove a file to the archive:

Zip File Header Details		
Offset	Bytes	Description
0	4	Local file header signature = 0x04034b50 (read as a little-endian no.)
4	2	Version needed to extract (minimum)
6	2	General purpose bit flag
8	2	Compression method
10	2	File last modification time
12	2	File last modification date
14	4	CRC-32
18	4	Compressed size
22	4	Uncompressed size
26	2	File name length (n)
28	2	Extra field length (m)
30	n	File name
30+n	m	Extra field

Reference-https://pkware.cachefly.net/webdocs/casestudies/APPNOTE.TXT

All the processes, actions taken, and files examined were duly documented and hashed. The copies were stored in a secure environment.

Based on the information gathered so far, the investigation team could infer a few pieces of information, as shown in the following:

- The attacker(s) had a strong insight into the organization hierarchy as well as the network architecture
- Sensitive data had been successfully collected from specific systems by person or persons unknown
- The data had been exfiltrated from the organizational network as recently as two days prior to the receipt of the e-mail
- The attacker(s) was/were technically savvy and quite aware of the security perimeter around the organization's network

Due to the time-sensitive nature of the exercise, it was decided to adopt a layered approach to the investigation process. Rather than trawling through tons of logs over many months, it was decided that a quick selective first phase would be initiated, followed by a full-fledged collection and analysis of the logs in order to identify the modus operandi of the attackers, understand the breach methodology, and suggest remedial measures.

As part of the initial evidence acquisition process, the following actions were taken:

- The logs for the past one month were collected, as follows:
  - Firewall
  - IPS/IDS
  - Proxy servers
  - DNS requests
  - Domain authentications
  - Anti-virus alerts
  - File access
  - E-mail server logs

- System memory image acquisition for four different systems was authorized. This included the CEO's system as well as the other three systems that were identified as the potential source of sensitive files sent to the CEO in the e-mail attachment.

- Media acquisition to create disk images of the three systems with sensitive files was authorized. This was to be done during the out-of-work hours to prevent anyone from being alerted about the investigation.

All the preceding information and evidence was forensically acquired for further analysis, with the explicit understanding that the process of analysis of the previously acquired data may reveal more clues that may lead us back to the acquisition stage where we may go about acquiring additional data and information that may have a bearing on our case.

For example, it was understood that a study of the acquired logs may help identify the system from where the exfiltration took place and an acquisition of the memory and media would be required to further the investigative process. Therefore, we need to keep in mind that this is an iterative process and we may be required to go back to gather further data based on the facts uncovered during the analysis phase.

Analyzing the collected data – digging deep

Analysis of the gathered data is a long and time-intensive process. As network forensic experts, we need to work towards the goals defined for us within the available time frame. In this specific case that we have been discussing, the situation is extremely time critical. Looking at the huge volume of potential evidence available to us, we have to take a call on the triaging process and decide what we wish to focus on first.

One very valuable input that we deduced was that the data had been exfiltrated just over two days before the receipt of the mail by the CEO. The process of exfiltration of data by any criminal actually involves a chain of events. These links in the chain or steps are shown in the following:

- Reconnaissance
- Compromise
- Setup of command and control
- Data identification, acquisition, and aggregation
- Exfiltration

While each of these stages will leave some traces on the victims systems, the major role of a forensics investigator comes into play during the last two stages.

Returning to our specific case, we are aware of an exfiltration having taken place. As exfiltration involves large volumes of data leaving the network, it becomes important to identify all the outbound network activity that relates to this in the specified time range. Therefore, logs from the proxy server are examined for the two-day period to identify, if possible, the exfiltration of about 500 MB or more of data. The figure of 500 MB is arrived at based on the contents of the mail received by the CEO, where the attacker had threatened to expose over 500 MB of sensitive data allegedly held by him. While there is no hard and fast rule that the attacker will exfiltrate the complete 500 MB in one go (this could be broken into more manageable packets, encrypted, and sent out all at once or over an extended period of time), if we refer back to the stages of an exfiltration-focused attack, we will find that exfiltration is the last and final stage. It is very common among attackers to accumulate the data and then try and upload the data out in one go due to the fear that the moment the data is identified as having left the network, all the previously used avenues for further data exfiltration will be shutdown and the process of remediation and recovery will be initiated. This is the stage that carries the highest risk of discovery for the criminal; once the discovery has been made, further opportunities to exfiltrate the data may be severely affected.

The proxy server logs provide the forensic investigator some interesting insights. The first observation made is that over the two-day period prior to the e-mail, there is not much activity. That is understandable due to it being a weekend. A study of the data that is transferred does not show any single large exfiltration of a file of that magnitude. While this rules out data exfiltration in a single shot, the possibility of data having been exfiltrated in segments still remains.

There is some HTTPS traffic in the logs that seems to carry the data that is close to 20 MB. However, this is encrypted and we are only able to see the basic metadata information such as source, destination, and port details. The following image graphically represents the path taken to exfiltrate data:

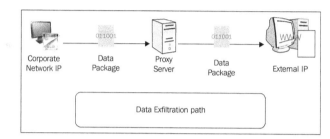

To begin with, we look closely at the logs associated with the suspected HTTPS traffic.

An examination of the logs shows that this traffic was directed to the `46.246.46.27` IP. An online lookup shows that this IP address belongs to an organization in Sweden. To perform this online lookup, we visit any site on the Web that allows us to do a Whois IP lookup. I use `https://whois.net/`. A whois query of the IP under investigation is shown as follows:

```
WHOIS Query For 46.246.46.27

% This is the RIPE Database query service.
% The objects are in RPSL format.
%
% The RIPE Database is subject to Terms and Conditions.
% See http://www.ripe.net/db/support/db-terms-conditions.pdf

% Note: this output has been filtered.
%       To receive output for a database update, use the "-B" flag.

% Information related to '46.246.32.0 - 46.246.63.255'

% Abuse contact for '46.246.32.0 - 46.246.63.255' is 'abuse@portlane.com'

inetnum:        46.246.32.0 - 46.246.63.255
netname:        PRIVACTUALLY-NET
descr:          Privactually Ltd
country:        SE
admin-c:        PN1967-RIPE
tech-c:         PN1967-RIPE
status:         ASSIGNED PA
mnt-by:         MNT-PORTLANE
created:        2013-03-20T14:38:50Z
last-modified:  2013-03-20T14:38:50Z
source:         RIPE # Filtered

role:           Portlane NOC
address:        BOX 134
address:        31122 Falkenberg
address:        Sweden
abuse-mailbox:  abuse@portlane.com
nic-hdl:        PN1967-RIPE
mnt-by:         MNT-PORTLANE
created:        2007-04-04T23:57:17Z
last-modified:  2015-09-04T08:06:03Z
source:         RIPE # Filtered
```

An attempt to connect to it in the incognito mode does not yield any result. Further research on the Internet shows multiple online lists that show this IP as a part of the Tor network, as shown in the following image:

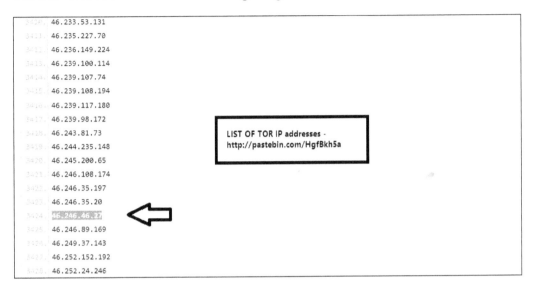

From the investigation perspective, this is a eureka moment. The e-mail that triggered this investigation originated from the Tor network. We now uncovered the logs that show some evidence of exfiltration to the Tor network. Ordinary users usually do not access Tor unless they have critical reasons for staying anonymous.

Now, having unknotted one end of the ball of string, the investigator proceeds to unravel the rest of the puzzle. Based on the organizational network architecture charts (made during the preparation stage in the earlier chapters), our investigator identifies the organizational IP address associated with the computer that was used as the staging post for the exfiltration. This turns out to be an old computer used as a print server in the organization.

All throughout the network forensic investigation process, the senior management team is kept appraised of the development and progress.

Following proper forensic procedures, a covert image of both the memory and media of the print server is made and preserved.

Based on the decisions made by the senior management, it is decided to disable the network connectivity to the print server while making the disruption seem part of a network outage.

In the meantime, a high speed examination of the forensic images that were created earlier is made.

A short summary of the relevant findings is listed in the following:

- The print server runs Windows 7 as its operating system.

- It has two logical drives, labeled C and D.

- The D drive has a folder path called `windows\system\print spooler`.

- In the folder, there are a large number of ZIP files that total to about 420 MB in compressed form.

- Each of these ZIP archives are password protected.

- However, the filenames of the files contained in the ZIP files can be seen and these correspond to sensitive files obtained from different parts of the organization.

- One ZIP archive is not password protected, this is the same ZIP file that was sent to the CEO via e-mail.

- An examination of the date and time stamps on these files show that the earliest archive was created about a month ago.

- Logs on the system are analyzed and it is established that the print server was regularly accessed using Windows **Remote Desktop Protocol (RDP)** during this period. These RDP logs are available, as per the following screenshot:

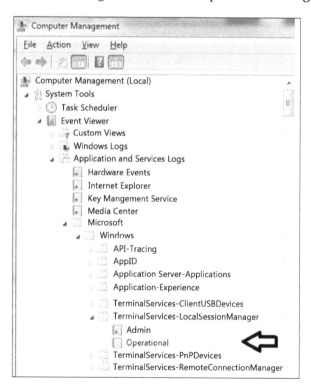

- Network admin credentials have been used for access.

- The computers used for access were those belonging to a common pool used by the IT support staff in the organization.

At this juncture, the picture was becoming a lot clearer. The evidence collected so far also pointed to an insider involvement. A picture of the adversary was emerging slowly and the need for caution and speed was increasing.

A schematic diagram depicting the data exfiltration route was made for better understanding of the incident. This is shown in the following:

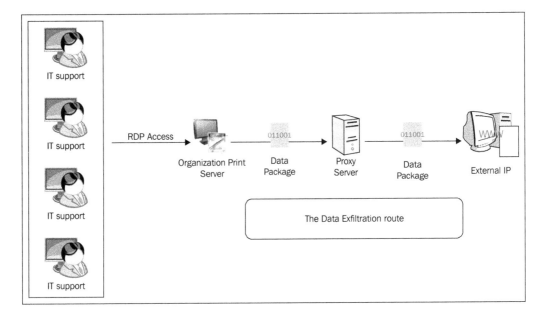

It was clear that an insider with administrator privileges could actually cause considerable harm to the organization and had to be removed at the earliest. However, this had to be done in a smooth manner so that the insider remained unaware right until the last minute. It was quite evident that, with network administrator privileges, the insider could be privy to all the e-mail conversations on the e-mail servers, administrator actions, as well as confidential data across the length and breadth of the network.

Therefore, the need for caution and speed!

Again, after a quick consultation, it was decided to once again enable the network access of the print server and perform a Wireshark capture for all the network traffic from and to that IP address.

However, to prevent the existing collected data from being exfiltrated, it was decided that the ZIP files lying on the print server would be damaged using a hex editor so that even in the event that they were exfiltrated, they would be corrupted and unusable. The idea was to gain some time and gather further the evidence, while every effort was made to identify the perpetrator at the earliest.

Keeping the preceding information as the prime objective, the CSO, working in parallel, called for the biometric access records in order to determine the people who had worked in the specified office over the weekend in question. Two IT support engineers were identified. He also called for their HR files to check their track records.

In the meantime, our Digital 007 covertly captured forensic images of memory and media of the suspected systems. Simultaneously, he looked further back in the log entries to determine other days and time that Tor had been accessed. The Tor access was correlated with the RDP access of the print server as well. A proper timeline of these activities was created. This was shared with the CSO for correlation with attendance and access records.

The result was that one of the IT support engineers fit directly in the slot. With clarity obtained, the immediate objective of identifying the attacker was achieved.

From the system images created, it was determined that the person in question was abusing his privileged position as an IT support engineer by disabling the protection on sensitive systems and deploying keyloggers to gather critical information as well as user credentials. A collection of malware was recovered as well as the evidence of having searched for *anonymous e-mail free* and other suggestive search terms that were indicative of his intentions.

Reporting the case

Once the iterative process of network forensic investigations is complete, the real tough part begins. This is the time when all the effort that was put in to maintain the meticulous documentation pays off.

Reporting a case is a lot like narrating a story. The only difference is that stories can be fictional or modified to create a better tale; whereas, an investigation report allows no such artistic liberty. It has to be thoroughly grounded in fact. Every statement should be backed by solid evidence. Every conjecture should be backed by circumstantial evidence and should be clearly identified as such.

A case report should be the following:

- Clear
- Concise
- Purposeful

Keep the audience that the case report is aimed at in mind. Very long reports are seldom read and the action points are hardly ever implemented, therefore, the structure is very important.

Most reports should begin with a case summary.

Following this, the report should at a minimum have the following structure:

- Introduction
- Information available and assumptions
- Investigations
- Findings
- Action taken and recommended

Recommendations need to be carefully thought out and should have a specific bearing on the network forensics aspect. Recommendations should include the following:

- Whether remediation should be initiated at the current time or not (this may have bearing on the fact that it may tip off the attacker and precipitate action that may be very damaging to the organization).

- Whether the scope of the assigned work should be narrowed or expanded to include more digital devices. A listing of additional possible sources of evidence should be made and provided to the management.

- Advice relating to the evidence-retention period should be taken from legal teams. This should form a part of the recommendations and additional secure storage should be arranged for this.

- If specific or new artifacts have been identified as part of the investigation and these can be used as a new IOC, the inclusion of these as IOC in the defense of the network should be recommended.

- Recommendations need also include actions that the organization is required to take as a part of legal or regulatory compliance. An example would be the finding of child pornography.

- Other than the preceding points, there are likely to be a number of case specific recommendations. All of these should be vetted and then presented to the management.

Action for the future

Once any incident is over and done with, the team needs to focus on the lessons learned. From an incident response perspective, the focus is on answering questions such as the following:

- How did this happen?
- What can we do to prevent it from reoccurring?
- What preventive measures can be put into place?
- How can monitoring and alerting be improved?

From a network forensics perspective, the additional questions to be answered include the following:

- Which artifacts exist that can help us identify such an incident in the future?
- What are the lessons learned?
- How can we improve the investigation process?
- What IOC can be identified that can be shared with the Incident Response team to help prevent a reoccurrence of such an incident?

While the attackers constantly evolve and innovate in order to keep coming up with newer ways to compromise the networks without getting detected, network forensic investigators too have to keep pace. This means constantly updating oneself, learning from peers, attending conferences and training programs, and so on. Rather than being in a reactive mode, it makes sense for the network forensic investigator to keep his eyes on the future.

Future of network forensics

While it is difficult to predict the future, some trends are self-evident. Let's take a look at them.

Organizations are moving to higher speed and bandwidth networks. More and more data is traveling over the networks and to and from a variety of devices.

IPv6 is here to stay! It brings along a proliferation of Internet-connected devices, right from your toaster, TV, refrigerator, photocopier, and coffee machine to your security and alarm system. This is known as the **Internet of Things** or **IoT** for short.

It does not require much crystal ball gazing to determine the trends of things to come in the network forensics domain. As a large number of devices get networked, there is going to be larger roles for Network Forensic 007s. We will be looking at more and more connected devices, the evidence that they store, the way that they act, and the way they are affected by different compromises. We will be collecting, handling, preserving, and analyzing large volumes of data.

Malware has already begun to evolve and will begin to target Internet-connected devices on a large scale, which may offer an easy entry point to organizational networks. It won't be long before we hear of hackers stealing data from a network by first compromising the office coffee machine.

We are also seeing an increasing trend of the data moving to the cloud. Network forensics will need to examine virtual IP addresses' activities on an enterprise scale to identify the activities that act as the IOC. Cloud forensics will be adjunct to network forensics.

As the threat scenario changes, security vendors all over the globe will enhance, upgrade, and innovate. New security products will hit the market. Network forensic investigators will need to learn new technologies and techniques to keep abreast of what is happening.

Summary

This final chapter sums up our journey in developing an understanding of network forensics. Along the way, we have seen myriad sources of evidence, artifacts created by attacker activities, as well as techniques and processes required to acquire and analyze them. You have learned how to put a report together to present our findings and also act upon your learning's from the investigation.

While this book acts as a starting point and helps in building a foundation in the network forensics area, remember that it is a big world out there and there is no end to the knowledge that one can and should gather as we boldly proceed forward in this field.

Thanks for being a part of this journey. I hope that it has been an interesting one and that I have been successful in kindling your interest in a very exciting new field.

Index

P

Packet Bytes pane 72
Packet Details pane 72
packet filter firewalls 169
Packet List pane 72
packet logger mode 124
packets
  broadcast 101
  multicast 101
  unicast 101
packet sniffing and analysis
  NetworkMiner used 78-84
  Wireshark used 69-78
passive and active sniffing
  on networks 67, 68
pattern matching 117
peer-to-peer (P2P) protocol 219
personally identifiable information
    (PII) 212
physical layer (PHY) 90
Point to Point Tunneling Protocol 188
Point to Point VPNs 184
Port Address Translation (PAT) 171
presentation layer 17
protocol, types
  carrier protocol 186
  encapsulating protocol 186
  passenger protocol 186
proxies
  about 153, 157-163
  servers 154
  types 154-157
proxies, types
  anonymizing proxy 155
  distorting proxy 156
  highly anonymizing proxy 155
  reverse proxy 157
  transparent proxy 156
PwC UK
  URL 10

Q

Quality of Service (QoS) 91

R

Ransomware 208, 209
Remote Access Server (RAS) 183
Remote Access VPNs 183
REMOTE_ADDR header 155
Remote Desk Protocol (RDP) 135
reverse proxy 157
RFC 1123 24
Rootkits 206, 207
routers 135, 176-179

S

Scumware
  URL 225
Secure Sockets Layer (SSL) 135
Secure Socket Tunneling Protocol 191
security logs
  about 134-136
  anti-virus/anti-malware software 134
  audit records 136
  authentication servers 136
  firewalls 135
  intrusion detection and prevention
    systems 135
  remote access software 135
  routers 135
  system events 136
  Uniform Resource Locators (URLs) 135
  vulnerability management software 136
seven-layer model
  about 16, 17
  TCP/IP model 17-19
Simple Network Markup Protocol
    (SNMP) 138
Single Carrier-Orthogonal frequency
    division multiplex (SC-OFDM) 92
small office or home office (SOHO)
    network 98
sniffer mode 123
SNORT
  network intrusion detection/prevention
    mode 125-127
  packet logger mode 124
  rule action, options 126
  rule header 126

Thank you for buying
Learning Network Forensics

About Packt Publishing

Packt, pronounced 'packed', published its first book, *Mastering phpMyAdmin for Effective MySQL Management*, in April 2004, and subsequently continued to specialize in publishing highly focused books on specific technologies and solutions.

Our books and publications share the experiences of your fellow IT professionals in adapting and customizing today's systems, applications, and frameworks. Our solution-based books give you the knowledge and power to customize the software and technologies you're using to get the job done. Packt books are more specific and less general than the IT books you have seen in the past. Our unique business model allows us to bring you more focused information, giving you more of what you need to know, and less of what you don't.

Packt is a modern yet unique publishing company that focuses on producing quality, cutting-edge books for communities of developers, administrators, and newbies alike. For more information, please visit our website at www.packtpub.com.

About Packt Open Source

In 2010, Packt launched two new brands, Packt Open Source and Packt Enterprise, in order to continue its focus on specialization. This book is part of the Packt Open Source brand, home to books published on software built around open source licenses, and offering information to anybody from advanced developers to budding web designers. The Open Source brand also runs Packt's Open Source Royalty Scheme, by which Packt gives a royalty to each open source project about whose software a book is sold.

Writing for Packt

We welcome all inquiries from people who are interested in authoring. Book proposals should be sent to author@packtpub.com. If your book idea is still at an early stage and you would like to discuss it first before writing a formal book proposal, then please contact us; one of our commissioning editors will get in touch with you.

We're not just looking for published authors; if you have strong technical skills but no writing experience, our experienced editors can help you develop a writing career, or simply get some additional reward for your expertise.

PACKT PUBLISHING

Learning Android Forensics

ISBN: 978-1-78217-457-8   Paperback: 322 pages

A hands-on guide to Android forensics, from setting up the forensic workstation to analyzing key forensic artifacts

1. A professional, step-by-step approach to forensic analysis complete with key strategies and techniques.

2. Analyze the most popular Android applications using free and open source tools.

3. Learn forensically-sound core data extraction and recovery techniques.

Learning iOS Forensics

ISBN: 978-1-78355-351-8   Paperback: 220 pages

A practical hands-on guide to acquire and analyze iOS devices with the latest forensic techniques and tools

1. Perform logical, physical, and file system acquisition along with jailbreaking the device.

2. Get acquainted with various case studies on different forensic toolkits that can be used.

3. A step-by-step approach with plenty of examples to get you familiarized with digital forensics in iOS.

Please check **www.PacktPub.com** for information on our titles

Practical Mobile Forensics

ISBN: 978-1-78328-831-1   Paperback: 328 pages

Dive into mobile forensics on iOS, Android, Windows, and BlackBerry devices with this action-packed, practical guide

1. Clear and concise explanations for forensic examinations of mobile devices.

2. Master the art of extracting data, recovering deleted data, bypassing screen locks, and much more.

3. The first and only guide covering practical mobile forensics on multiple platforms.

Kali Linux Cookbook

ISBN: 978-1-78328-959-2   Paperback: 260 pages

Over 70 recipes to help you master Kali Linux for effective penetration security testing

1. Recipes designed to educate you extensively on the penetration testing principles and Kali Linux tools.

2. Learning to use Kali Linux tools, such as Metasploit, Wire Shark, and many more through in-depth and structured instructions.

3. Teaching you in an easy-to-follow style, full of examples, illustrations, and tips that will suit experts and novices alike.

Please check **www.PacktPub.com** for information on our titles

www.ingramcontent.com/pod-product-compliance
Lightning Source LLC
Chambersburg PA
CBHW060530060326
40690CB00017B/3442